# BUILD *for* BETTER

The Practical Guide to Building
Digital Companies, Products and Teams

## BY JT WHITE

**BIS**PUBLISHERS

For permissions, inquiries, or additional resources, contact:
buildforbetterbook@gmail.com

**Published by:**
*BIS Publishers*
Timorplein 46
1094 CC Amsterdam
The Netherlands
bis@bispublishers.com
www.bispublishers.com

*Dedicated to the loving memory of my first Mom, Deb White. She always wanted to write a book and so much of who I am is because of who she was. If anything I wrote here can inspire anyone even one-hundredth as much as you continue to inspire me, this was all worth it.*

# Contents

The company you build, the culture you build, is just another product.

And you need to approach it in the exact same way you approach building things in the digital world.

# Setting The Stage: Unlocking the Secrets of Product Success

**1**

W hen I first set out to write this book, it was intended to be a guide to understanding and becoming a Product Manager for the digital age. I was tired of trying to explain to people what it was that I actually did for work. More than that, though, I was tired of how drastically different Product roles could be from company to company. And I wrote that book. All of it.

What happened next was frustrating. I realized that most of what I'd written about, most of what I was most passionate about, was building the relationships, the teams, and the culture where great products can be built—even more than the products themselves. But then I realized that the company you build, the culture you build, is just another product. And you need to approach it in the exact same way you approach building things in the digital world.

Building a digital product and company is f\*\*king hard. Really, really hard. Making it even harder is the complete lack of understanding on how to go about actually building either one from all the angles one must consider. Equally difficult is that there is a plethora of processes and methodologies that you are told you should use to be successful but often with little reason other than "big companies have succeeded building digital things this way," which is a shit reason.

The past thirty years have seen disruption in the form of technological advancement in a way that we have never seen before. From net new inventions to the furthering of what was groundbreaking technology just ten years ago, businesses, and therefore their employees, have had to radically transform the way they approach problems. The roles and responsibilities of organizations and people alike are vastly different now from what they have been in the past.

In this version of this book, we will focus on the people charged with owning whatever your core product is, and the processes that built that product. That could take the form of Entrepreneurs, CEOs, COOs, Product Development, Product Management, Product Innovation, or any other nonsense title you might want to assign to someone who is trying to build something. The impetus for writing this book is not that we don't have good digital companies, products, or process, because in lots of cases we do. But how we approach building them from their very conception to launch is being done in a way that has not evolved to match the companies and products themselves. I would argue we have good digital products more out a lack of great digital products to reference. So, I wanted to look at how we do things to better understand why we are where we are.

We will explore the history of building things to understand the reasons behind the process today, explore the perception and the realities of being in charge of building a digital product and the associated actors and roles, and arrive at a place where we can have better conversations as for how to push forward into a truly digital world where our process more directly mimics our products.

This book is written the way I and almost all of my colleagues and collaborators talk—like real people. I have read far too many business books that stand on ceremony and standard procedure instead of being transparent and honest. What does that actually mean? It means the following pages will be infused with curse words and likely far too many metaphors and oddly placed cultural references. This is done with great intention. It is time we stop taking ourselves so seriously and instead allow ourselves to be who we are. If any of the above gives you pause and offends your sensibilities, I tell you with great confidence that this book is not for you, so put it down. If you can handle a few adult words and want to get into the mud of how to have our business practices match our potential output, buckle in.

The glamorous 'Mad Men' view of sales culture is one of drinks and dinner, golf outings, and taking clients to shows where you simply reach into your illustrious toolkit and pull out a perfectly fitting object to solve their problem.

But the truth is quite the opposite.

# The Origin Story: Crafting a Book to Change How You View the Word "Product"

2

I lovingly refer to myself as an "Accidental Product Manager." I started my career in sales and truly believed it was what I was meant to do. I have always had a love of people and the process of getting to a place of truly understanding what it is a person needs.

Herein lay my issue. The glamorous "Mad Men" view of sales culture is one of drinks and dinner, golf outings and taking clients to shows where you simply reach into your illustrious toolkit and pull out a perfectly fitting object to solve their problem. But the truth is quite the opposite. More often than not, I found myself in a "square peg round hole" scenario rather than "let me wrap this up for you." So, in the absence of a perfectly manufactured out-of-the-box fix, I found myself constantly trying to force multiple products into a single one that was a better fit for my clients.

As I have come to learn after ten-plus years building digital products, those kinds of salespeople are both the biggest asset you have at your disposal and the very specific reason you take up drinking.

By always pushing the edges of products I was constantly putting pressure on the organization to build and maintain subsets of quality products on top of the "core" offering. But as I was always assigned a vertical or territory to which I needed to sell, I was left asking myself, "Why do we have this client segment if we don't have products they actually want to use?" or more selfishly, "How am I supposed to hit my goals with this garbage my customers can't use?"

I was lucky enough to have the faith (and mostly patience) of multiple leaders who allowed me to venture into the world of creating solutions for my customers based on truly defining their needs and then having the resources to build those solutions out for larger consumption.

The first product I ever built was a website for online rap battles. I was sixteen and an avid hip-hop fan. Chat rooms and bulletin boards were just becoming the norm online. I moved frequently as a kid and often I found myself an outcast among my peers. The internet allowed me to connect with like-minded people and build a community from afar. When my favorite hip-hop website became overcrowded and impossible to navigate, a friend of mine from the site and I decided to build our very own playground and invite only our favorite people. We used out-of-the-box VBulletin software and slowly built a small community of underground artists and fans. Eventually I was able to sell the site as a test bed for up-and-coming artists. I made no money off the sale, and the only lesson I learned at the time was that the music industry was awful. But it struck a chord in me.

Since that time, I have built just about every iteration of a digital product you can imagine. I launched websites and streaming services for local radio stations. I worked on authenticated TV Everywhere applications (streaming apps). I built the Travel Channel app for the AndroidTV launch at Google IO. I helped shape and launch self-service big data solutions for the largest content creators in the world. My team and I built a fully baked digital video ad server, data management platform, and order management system in service of in-app mobile video. I have worked tirelessly building data science-driven inventory and yield management software for cable operators and networks. And most recently I co-founded a company building an AI Assisted Video creation platform.

I have worked with teams of fifty-plus people and with teams that could sit on a single couch with room to spare. I have worn every hat, had absurd titles, worked with collocated teams, and have worked remotely. The only constant that I have found is that the best and worst leaders I have worked with all came from different paths, had different skill sets, and none of them had a blueprint for how they got to where they are.

With all the things I have built, I have had tremendous successes and abject failures. But what never wavered was my desire to service salespeople and/or consumers through the process of building things. While I always found success in negotiating scopes of work and contracts, it always felt as though I could, and should, be focusing on what was delivered and its effectiveness more than how and how much it was delivered for and in what amount of time. So, I have since dedicated my entire career to better servicing the needs of the people who use the products I create. Outside of my family, there is little that brings me as much joy as seeing something my team and I have created being enjoyed in the wild.

If you identify with any of the things I have said above, or if you are simply curious to find out if being a builder of digital companies and/or products is interesting to you, then the pages of this book will serve as a guide to doing so and will help you make decisions faster, avoid mistakes, and ask better questions right out of the gate.

Whether or not I should be looked to for advisement is subjective. I do not claim to be a "product whisperer," and I can tell you with a high level of confidence that anyone who says they are likely isn't. What I can promise you is that no book is going to give you all the answers. The beauty of creating products is that each one is special and its own. The best you can hope for—what you should hope for—out of this and any other reference, is guiding principles and practices to look to in those moments when you feel completely underwater. (They're coming, I promise.) The words on these pages are for you to take and apply as you see fit, and they exist because I would have killed to have them at my disposal during the past twenty-or-so years of my career.

The best you can hope for—what you should hope for—out of this and any other reference, is guiding principles and practices to look to in those moments when you feel completely underwater.

The fact that so much of what we do today comes from industries and verticals so far removed from where we live is telling.

# From Then to Now: Unveiling the Product Creation Journey

**3**

B efore we talk building digital products and companies, it's important to get an understanding of how non-digital products have been built for years. In establishing an understanding of the processes and procedures that have gone into creating the products that preceded the digital age, we will set the stage for why we approach things the way we do today.

What follows is a timeline of sorts as to how Product Management, and therefore the process of building products in general, came to exist. It's important context to have and will prove to be surprisingly beneficial to understand when you find yourself in the trenches of a build. It will become evident quickly that the overlap among many of the philosophies and methodologies is astounding and potentially might even feel repetitive. But as it is in the nature of a good Product Leader to be curious, learning how we arrived where we are today will help you with the decisions you will be required to make when it comes to how you approach assembling and managing your own teams in the future. The fact that so much of what we do today comes from industries and verticals so far removed from where we live is telling. But stripping away the "what" behind all that follows and focusing on the "why" is what will bring you the most benefit.

So, I implore you, don't skim over this part. Understanding it will shape the way you read everything else in this book and give you insight and appreciation you otherwise would not have. The journey that our predecessors went on ultimately led to the creation of the entire digital world, so while the practices and policies are ripe for change, the odyssey taken to arrive at this point is more meaningful than you might assume. And if nothing else, having this information at the ready will make you sound researched and professional when you inevitably have to explain to your parents or partner what the hell is it you actually do for a living.

## MASTERING EFFICIENCY: INSIGHTS FROM THE TOYOTA PRODUCTION SYSTEM

By most accounts Neil. H. McElroy, an executive of Proctor and Gamble (P&G) in the early 1930's, eventual United States Secretary of Defense, and one of the founding members of NASA, is the father of modern-day Product Management. McElroy had more work than he and his team could handle and was in need of more bodies. He wanted those bodies to be closer to the action, and was looking for insight from people who understood the entity of the value chain—from the product itself, to distribution, all the way to the end consumer. He called this role a "Brand Man." In 1931 he penned an 800-word document that outlined the following as the roles and responsibilities of such a person:

C
O
P    MARKETING
Y    - Brand Teams, 1931

cc: Mr. W. G. Werner

Mr. N. H. McElroy    May 13, 1931

Mr. R. F. Rogan

ADV**N. H. MCELROY

Because I think it may be of some help to you in cutting through our recommendation for additional men for the Promotion Department, I am outlining briefly below the duties and responsibilities of the brand men.

This outline does not represent the situation as it is but as we will have it when we have sufficient man power. In past years the brand men have been forced to do work that should have been passed on to assistant brand men, if they had been available and equal to the job.

Brand Man

(1) Study carefully shipments of his brands by units.

(2) Where brand development is heavy and where it is progressing, examine carefully the combination of effort that seems to be clicking and try to apply this same treatment to other territories that are comparable.

(3) Where brand development is light

 (a) Study the past advertising and promotional history of the brand; study the territory personally at first hand - both dealers and consumers - in order to find out the trouble.
 (b) After uncovering our weakness, develop a plan that can be applied to this local sore spot. It is necessary, of course, not simply to work out the plan but also to be sure that the amount of money proposed can be expected to produce results at a reasonable cost per case.
 (c) Outline this plan in detail to the Division Manager under whose jurisdiction the weak territory is, obtain his authority and support for the corrective action.

21

**I.**   Study carefully shipments of his brands by units.

**II.**   Where brand development is heavy and where it is progressive, examine carefully the combination of effort that seems to be clicking and try to apply this same treatment to other territories that are comparable.

**II.**   Where brand development is light:

**(a)**   Keep whatever records are necessary and make whatever field studies are necessary to determine whether the plan has produced the expected results.

**(b)**   Study past advertising and promotional history of the brand: study the territory personality at first hand—both dealers and consumers—in order to find out the trouble.

**(c)**   After uncovering our weakness, develop a plan that can be applied to this local sore spot. It is necessary, of course, not simply to work out the plan but also to be sure that the amount of money proposed can be expected to produce results at a reasonable cost per case.

**(d)**   Outline this plan in detail to the Division Manager under whose jurisdiction the weak territory is, obtain his authority and support for the corrective action.

**(e)**   Prepare sales help and all other necessary material for carrying out the plan. Pass it on to the districts. Work with salesmen while they are getting started.

**(f)**   Follow through to the very finish to be sure that there is no letdown in sales operation of the plan.

IV.  Take full responsibility, not simply for criticizing individual pieces of printed word copy, but also for the general printed word plans for his brands.

V.   Take full responsibility for all other advertising expenditures on his brands.

VI.  Experiment with and recommend wrapper revisions.

VII. See each District Manager a number of times a year to discuss with him any possible faults in our promotion plans for that territory."

What McElroy keyed into that had not yet been truly actualized was the power of direct contact with the consumer, through the eyes of a business-minded individual, to influence the development of the actual products. This predates the founding of Focus Groups (a child of Robert Merton in 1946) or any other direct link to consumers beyond trials.

So, in essence, what McElroy is approaching here is the idea of User-Centric Development (an idea and word construct we will tackle later). His belief in this need and influence did not end here. McElroy was also an advisor at Stanford, where he is said to have had a heavy influence on Bill Hewlett and David Packard, eventual founders of Hewlett Packard and champions of letting customers drive development.

# TOYOTA PRODUCTION SYSTEM (TPS)

In the 1950s, postwar Japan was experiencing issues in delivering products due to lack of cashflow and access to material. This forced manufacturers to build in new, more efficient ways to meet consumer needs. This need fostered the birth of the Toyota Production System (TPS). TPS was created by Taiichi Ohno and Eiji Toyoda. Eiji was the nephew of Toyota's founder, Kiichiro Toyoda, and would later become the Chief Executive and Chairman of the company. TPS was the marriage of ancient principles in Japanese culture, Kaizen and Genchi.

Kaizen (改善) is the Sino-Japanese word for "improvement." Genchi Genbutsu (現地現物) translates to "go and see for yourself." So, the literal combination of these two concepts is to continually improve through observation.

For Taiichi and Eiji, this became a way of life for Toyota. By being on the ground floor of not only the people using their product but the people building them as well, Toyota built a process that entirely changed the way companies approached product development. There are two standouts from TPS that are still the basis for how many products are built today.

I.  The introduction of the PDCA (Plan, Do, Check, and Act) process. This process has taken many forms over the years. It is called the Deming circle/cycle/wheel, the Shewhart cycle, the control circle/cycle, the plan–do–study–act (PDSA), or you can add "Observation" and get the OPDCA. For any of you who took science in middle school, this should sound relatively familiar, as it is a consolidated version of the Scientific Method.

But no matter what name you assign to it, the steps remain relatively consistent:

- Create a hypothesis or premise you are going to solve and clearly state how you intend to solve it.
- Perform tests to evaluate if what you thought was right, documenting throughout the process where and how things did or did not work.
- Change your original statement or approach to reflect the changes you observed during the "Check" stage. This is also where if, your idea was horrible, you can decide to save yourself a tremendous amount of heartache and just let it be a horrible idea and walk away.
- Start the process over again with your new understanding and approach.

The idea of a Kanban board. While the name might not ring a bell for most, I promise you that you have seen one of these before. A Kanban board is quite literally a board where you break out the different vertical columns of work, stage by stage, and then create tasks associated with building the larger product. Traditionally, every task will start all the way to the left and work its way to the right. It is intended to allow Product Owners to keep track of where tasks are in the development lifecycle and ensure that dependencies and deliverables are on track. It is intended to be open and collaborative, much in the spirit of Kaizen, continually improving the process and the communication around the process as well. In the world today, hundreds of millions of dollars are spent annually on toolsets which allow companies to track product development via the Kanban board.

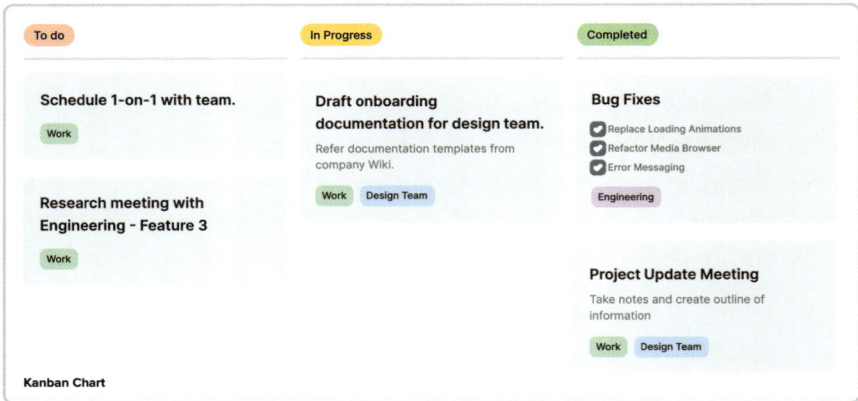

Kanban Chart

Well into the 1980s, these two, along with many other principles of Toyota Production System, guided the building of products, and therefore heavily influenced the creation of company culture. From automobiles to furniture to appliances, TPS created a true north for how to approach building things in a way that minimized churn, increased efficiency, and put creators closer to their users. It is directly responsible for all the methods that follow it and is the reason we have the kind of products we have today.

## SIX SIGMA DEMYSTIFIED: ACHIEVING EXCELLENCE IN PRODUCTION

After the rampant success of TPS, American and European companies adopted the practice, giving it their own twists to suit it more to cultural norms, or just renaming it and saying it was theirs. One of the big breakthroughs that did come from TPS (thirty-some-odd years later) was the development of Six Sigma.

In 1980, Bill Smith, an American engineer working at Motorola, introduced a set of tools focused on process improvement. The term "Six Sigma process" comes from the notion that if one has six standard deviations between the process mean and the nearest specification limit, practically no items will fail to meet specifications. This is based on the calculation method employed in process capability studies.

Six Sigma was built around the previously mentioned Deming's Plan-Do-Act-Study concept, specifically employing two different versions of the methodology:

I.  DMAIC – Define, Measure, Analyze, Improve, Control

- Define the system, the voice of the customer and their requirements, and the project goals, specifically.

- Measure key aspects of the current process and collect relevant data; calculate the "as-is" Process Capability.

- Analyze the data to investigate and verify cause-and-effect relationships. Determine what the relationships are and attempt to ensure that all factors have been considered. Seek out the root cause of the defect under investigation.

- Improve or optimize the current process based upon data analysis using techniques such as design of experiments, Poka-yoke (a Japanese term for mistake proofing), and standard work to create a new, future state process. Set up pilot runs to establish process capability.

- Control the future state process to ensure that any deviations from the target are corrected before they result in defects. Implement control systems such as statistical process control, production boards, visual workplaces, and continuously monitor the process. This process is repeated until the desired quality level is obtained.

II.    DMADV – Define, Measure, Analyze, Design, Verify

- Define design goals that are consistent with customer demands and the enterprise strategy.
- Measure and identify CTQs (characteristics that are Critical to Quality), measure product capabilities, production process capability, and measure risks.
- Analyze to develop and design alternatives.
- Design an improved alternative, best suited per analysis in the previous step.
- Verify the design, set up pilot runs, implement the production process, and hand it over to the process owner(s).

While Six Sigma was created at Motorola, it was General Electric (GE) that truly brought it to the masses. In 1995, Jack Welch, Chairman and CEO of GE from 1981 to 2001, adopted Six Sigma as a standard practice for the whole company. As part of the adoption, GE created certification programs within the organization. Drafting off the original Japanese influence of Six Sigma, they used "belts" to signify where in the certification process an employee was. Much like in the Japanese martial arts, you started as a white belt, and as you moved through the process, could eventually become a black belt. The concept of a Six Sigma black belt became a cross-industry sign of respect and admiration, creating a whole new order of consultants labeled as "black belts," who would promise to come in and clean up your organization's process. It became standard practice for "black belts" to teach companies the way of Six Sigma, increasing the output of product companies.

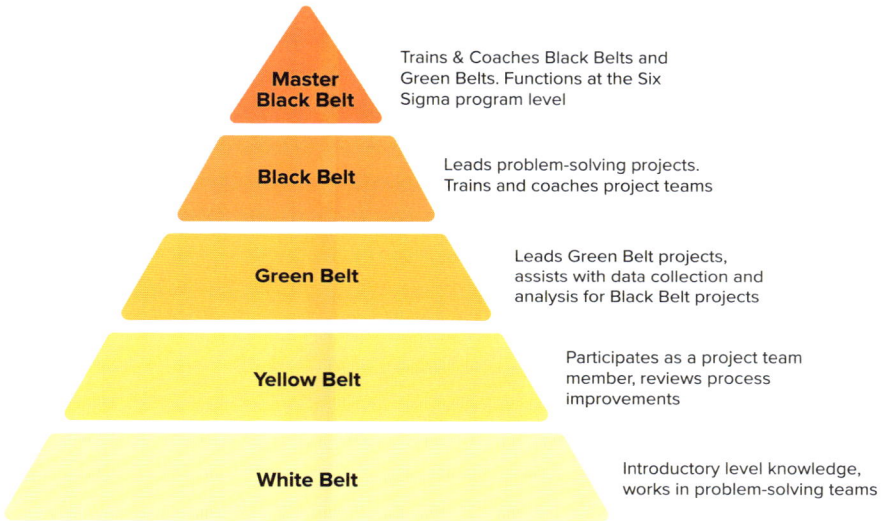

Where TPS focused on users and the general output, Six Sigma was much more internally process focused. The goal of Six Sigma is to reduce waste and increase efficiency in how you build products themselves, but in doing so, it allows products to have a certain level of defect (99.99966 percent is the goal for successful Six Sigma.) By many accounts, Six Sigma was simply a lightweight, easy to understand Quality Assurance practice that focused more on speed of production than quality itself.

Regardless of what you think about Six Sigma as a practice, it absolutely shaped the way products were created and has had a lasting effect on how we approach things even in the digital age. The focus on continual improvement of the internal processes as much as the product itself was a mind shift. Whether people looked for true efficiency or to cut corners to save time and cost, its influence is everlasting.

## THE ESSENTIALS OF LEAN MANAGEMENT

Lean manufacturing, or Lean production, is a systematic method originating in the Japanese manufacturing industry for the minimization of waste (無駄 muda) within a manufacturing system without sacrificing productivity, which can cause problems.

The actual practice of "Lean" manufacturing and thinking goes back far before TPS was a concept. You can trace Lean principles all the way back to Benjamin Franklin's Poor Richard's Almanac, where he states, "He that idly loses 5s worth of time, loses 5s, and might as prudently throw 5s into the river." But it wasn't until TPS that the concept of Lean was truly enacted in a repeatable, definable way.

There are entire books about Lean practices, most famously The Lean Startup by Eric Ries, which for many was a bible of sorts for starting a company in the digital age. He goes into great detail about his approach and implementation of Lean practices to create a company and product that is set up for success. It's a good read—buy it.

Unlike TPS or Six Sigma, I am not going to break down Lean quite as thoroughly. The reason for this is that it cannot be done successfully. "Lean" has come to mean different things to different people depending on industry, title, and willingness to engage in conversation about it.

What we can and will discuss is what ALL the different methods are actually trying to achieve and why they can be good or bad for your product and company.

The very word itself tells a large portion of the story. Merriam-Webster defines "lean" as "lacking or deficient in flesh" or "containing little or no fat." What that reads like to me, and likely to many who have worked within a Lean organization before, is "do more with less."

There is a fine line between efficiency and insanity when it comes to building a product, and it's one that requires you as the Product Owner to pay very close attention. Due to the overinflation of valuations and the complete lack of knowledge as to what the digital world would be, bloat has been a real issue for companies in the industry. The practice of hiring people as rapidly as possible when you could became commonplace in the early digital world, stemming mostly from the age-old saying "I would rather have it and not need it than need it and not have it." But years of this weighed on investors and inventors alike, creating a culture where Lean became a buzzword and a must-have for companies in the 2010's, so much so that being Lean became a prerequisite for every investor pitch deck.

The truth is, Lean just came to mean "efficient and appropriately staffed." You could check all the Lean boxes and never once use a single practice from the documented methodologies. And that's actually fine.

The lesson in Lean for product and company owners is really a simple one, but also of enormous gravity—know what the f**k you are building and plan accordingly. If you operate your company or your product in a manner that is not "lean," you aren't paying attention, or you don't actually know what you are trying to build. Later on in the book I will discuss focus in greater detail, but that is the lesson that is still being learned from "Lean management and manufacturing principles." Digital was so far from Lean out of the gate that we overcorrected over time and now don't ask what is reasonable and right but instead "How far can we push this before it explodes." With that in mind, I refer back to the first definition from Webster's—"lacking or deficient in flesh." Read that as dying . . .

## THE AGILE AND CONTINUOUS DEVELOPMENT EVOLUTION

Agile and Continuous Development are related more specifically to, well, development than they are to building the products themselves, but they deserve a callout here. As the digital world advances, we have evolved the business practices that allow us to build the products we create. Both the idea of "Agile" and "Continuous" development is the engineering answer to moving away from Lean principles and moving toward practices that more directly relate to the digital world.

"Agile" was coined in 2001 when the "Manifesto for Agile Software Development" was created by seventeen software engineers at a retreat in Snowbird, Utah. The concept was not new, as it was preceded by RAD (rapid application development), UP (Unified Process), and scrum (a framework within which people can address complex adaptive problems while productively and creatively delivering products of the highest possible value), among others. However, the "Manifesto for Agile Software Development" was the pivotal moment.

Agile development stands on the following values:

I.     Individuals and Interactions over processes and tools

II.   Working Software over comprehensive documentation

III.  Customer Collaboration over contract negotiation

IV.   Responding to Change over following a plan

"Manifesto for Agile Software Development" furthered the above by adding the following principles:

I.    Customer satisfaction by early and continuous delivery of valuable software.

II.   Welcome changing requirements, even in late development.

III.  Deliver working software frequently (weeks rather than months).

IV.   Close, daily cooperation between businesspeople and developers.

V.    Projects are built around motivated individuals, who should be trusted.

VI.   Face-to-face conversation is the best form of communication (co-location).

VII.  Working software is the primary measure of progress.

VIII. Sustainable development, able to maintain a constant pace.

IX.   Continuous attention to technical excellence and good design.

X.    Simplicity—the art of maximizing the amount of work not done—is essential.

XI.   Best architectures, requirements, and designs emerge from self-organizing teams.

**XII.** Regularly, the team reflects on how to become more effective, and adjusts accordingly.

For a process that skews toward action over documentation, it is very well documented. But what Agile functionally did that was meaningful was move away from the "waterfall" style that most companies leveraged to build. The idea of a waterfall was that it was clearly sequential; you build A first, then B, then C, constantly cascading and always thinking through the correct order. With the value and principles listed above, Agile pushed for a more flexible, adaptive style of development. This was a huge change and flew in the face of many of the previously mentioned practices (think about applying Six Sigma principles to a process that is evolving in real time—headaches and LOTS of very upset consultants).

Whether through necessity or a happy accident based on the technology available, the Agile process also brought product companies and product people closer to the users again. The focus on "super serving" the user was heading back to what TPS originally set out to do and away from the internal concentration on "efficiency or die." This more holistic look at what was being built, and willingness to amend that as feedback came in from both users and the development team, drastically changed the landscape for the better.

The other differentiator that Agile introduced, which is paramount to the success of any digital solution, is cross-team collaboration. In much of the physical product world, teams are allowed to, and can succeed, working in complete silos. Think about the manufacturing of cell phones. There is an internal antenna in every one of them. The team that creates that antenna is given hard requirements around range, size, and material. It designs them, produces them, and ships them for assembly. Once they are done, they are done. Nothing can be changed, amended, or moved. If mistakes were made, heads roll, and you start over.

This is clearly not the case in the digital world. Because the products we build are not physical, we can make changes, introduce new concepts or features, or even pivot an entire idea into a new lane as needed. But doing so requires alignment WELL before any action is taken. I will discuss the relationships required to build a great digital product later, but it demands attention in this part of the conversation as well. By sharing not only line of sight but also deliverables, the Agile environment forces cross-team communication in a way that its predecessors did not.

Continuous Development (CD) takes Agile a step even further. While Agile's intention is to be more malleable, it still has frequent stops to make the software you build ready to be released, most commonly done in windows that are referred to as "Sprints." A Sprint is a set period of time during which specific work has to be completed and made ready for review and release. Continuous Development asks Engineers to build software in such a way that it is ready for rapid release without any stopping.

It's important to distinguish here that Continuous Development is not about making things faster or recklessly, it's about the elimination of the step of "cleansing" or "preparing" the code for release. It is also worth calling out that there is a difference between being READY to be released and actually being pushed into production. But I digress.

The reason I bring these two concepts up in this context is because in order to understand how to build a digital product successfully, you need to understand why and how things are built today. In the digital world we have a tendency to fall in love with ideas, concepts, and best practices and make them gospel across the board. The fact is that, depending on your product and your team, it's unlikely any one of the methods just discussed is the perfect one. It is likely an amalgamation of a few, or perhaps even all of them, that will get you and your team where you need to go. But walking in without the context of why each of these exists, or assuming that you need to or should build your product using one of these because anyone other than you and your team thinks it's the right thing to do, is shortsighted and foolish. Do the research, talk with your team, and establish a process and cadence, based on history AND your personal needs, to figure out how best to work.

## THE BIG WHY: CONNECTING THE DOTS IN BUILDING DIGITAL PRODUCTS

Philosophy, that's why.

In building your company, your culture, and your product, every decision you make has an impact on your overall philosophy. In some instances, these things are written down, shared with your teams, and pointed to as north stars. Very often, what's written is aspirational, not real. Your real company philosophy plays out in your culture much more than in the "pillars" on your website.

The most important thing to remember, whatever choices you make around philosophy, is that you can and should change it as you build. Wedding yourself to something because it felt like a good idea when you thought of it rarely ends well (see: communism—brilliant on paper but flawed due to lack of accounting for the human condition). You and your team should not be mandated to do anything other than deliver on the promises of the product you sign up for. If you are a CEO or an Entrepreneur, it will serve you well to remember that as you assemble your team. If you are a product professional and in an environment where you do not have the choice to change the process to best suit your product and team, look around and be sure you love what you're building. Ultimately, working at big companies might not allow for this, but more and more companies are giving autonomy to Product Owners who are bold enough to ask for it, as delivery of meaningful products should be the goal, not a case study in process.

The only tried and true way to become a good product person is to become a product person.

# The Anatomy of a Product: Understanding Its Core

## 4

As the digital world has exploded, the very concept of what is a "product" has become increasingly more fluid. If you met two people who identified themselves as "Product Leaders in the digital space," you would likely have no idea what they did, and even if you were to guess, you would probably be wrong. To add another layer of complexity to that scenario, if you asked them both to describe what they did, it could genuinely be two completely different things. "Digital" is a catchall word that doesn't actually give you any sense of what it means.

In the physical world, we tend to be able to more easily understand what a product is. If you are at a dinner party and meet someone who builds furniture, you have a pretty firm grasp on what they do. Now the truth is that "building furniture" could mean any number of things. Commercial? Residential? What kind of material does the person use? Are they a woodworker or a welder? Do they subscribe to a certain design aesthetic or time period? But for the most part, knowing you build furniture is enough to stop the conversation at a dinner party.

Now take that same example and insert "I build digital products." If you do build digital products, it's very likely you have heard this as a follow-up: "So you build apps"? Even that concept opens a can of worms, because the word "apps" likely doesn't mean what that person thinks it means. So many of us will just say "yes" or find a way to point to something the person likely knows of and say, "Kind of like that."

If you really want to blow someone's mind, explain the number of digital products that exist in some of their favorite physical products. Let's use a smart TV as a touchstone.

When you turn the smart TV on, you are activating its operating system (digital product). From there, there's also a user interface which allows you to interact with certain aspects of that operating system—audio and video settings, input labeling, etc. (digital products). Then your smart TV has applications you can use to access your content. For the sake of ease, let's assume there are only three: Netflix, Sling TV, and Pandora (each one a stand-alone digital product). But here comes the fun part—did you know that within each of those digital products is a whole litany of other digital products? Netflix and Sling TV don't write all those synopses themselves; they source that metadata from third parties who sell it to them. All the cover art in Pandora's library—you guessed it: digital product. The recommendation engines that drive what you listen to or watch next—some might be proprietary, but they could also be a digital product.

So, when you turn on your smart TV to sit down and engage in the simple pleasures of some nightly entertainment, in the extremely limited example above you could be activating—at the very least—eight digital products in order to do so. Eight products.

The main difference in the physical and digital world is that so many digital products are truly invisible. In the physical world you might have to dig deep to find all the little pieces that make up a larger product, but you can ultimately see them. Watches are my favorite example.

A single Patek Philippe watch can contain as many as 1,300 pieces and twenty complications. Each of those complications is a kind of stand-alone product that does something other than tell time. It can be as simple as keeping the date or as sophisticated as a tourbillion, which is a rotating cage that the escapement and balance wheel (the things that do keep time) are located within to negate the effects of gravity when the timepiece is stuck in a certain position. You don't need to understand watches any further to understand the concept, which is that lots of physical products rely on other, smaller products to make them work. But in the physical world you can reasonably assess how a product comes together.

In the digital world it is much harder. Many of the digital products being produced today have no physical manifestation at all. From the aforementioned metadata streams that fuel your decision-making on TV, the ever mocked "cloud" storage systems that keep all your memes and selfies at the ready, or the aggressively creepy facial recognition technology in Google photos that creates albums for you, the number of "invisible" digital products that we use daily would astound most people.

Even for those of us that live and breathe the space, keeping tabs on all the different players and technologies that feed into the more visible digital products is an insurmountable task. The very best of us might be able to keep straight a particular business vertical, but as quickly as things change in digital, even that can be a fruitless effort.

As we will discuss in length later, the only person that truly matters in creating digital products is the end user, and the truth is the vast majority of them couldn't be bothered in the least to know the inner workings of all the products they use. If it works for them, they are happy. So, with that in mind, let's make this as simple and academic as possible.

Merriam-Webster defines a product simply as "something produced" or "something (such as a service) that is marketed or sold as a commodity." As should be the case when defining an individual product itself, these simple, straightforward, and concise definitions will work just fine for our purposes.

If it's something you create, regardless of whether it can be seen or accessed directly or even understood or acknowledged by most users, let's all agree to call it a product.

## FROM PRACTICE TO PERFECTION: THE ART OF PRODUCT CRAFTING

In a landscape that still puts great stock in pedigree and training, there are still no universally recognized programs, be they independent or collegiate, that "teach" Product Leadership/Management or how to actually build products in the digital age. In my opinion, this is exactly as it should be. As we will discuss later in the book, there is no archetype for what would make a good Product Owner.

Coming from sales worked for me because of the actual art of selling. Much of how I work is getting buy-in from both the executers and the receivers of a product that what we are doing is meaningful and that we can have fun while doing it. So much of building a product is about salesmanship internally before you ever even have the chance to put it in front of your end users. Learning how to navigate a room full of people who know you are pitching them and getting them on board anyway is a skill set that will help anyone in life, not just in developing a successful digital product.

With all the benefits of a sales background, there are also glaring omissions. For one, salespeople tend to not love the word "no," which needs to be a word you are super comfortable with as a Product Owner. The desire to please everyone and be liked is often not synonymous with Product Owners, and for good reason. The other obvious issue is that generally you need to have some technical awareness in order to get things done. I will address this later, but it is an important callout, as the number of environments in which having no technical understanding will suffice is limited.

If you come from a technical background (as more and more Product people do) you can take a much more tactical, engineering-focused approach to problem-solving. I have found that in my career most Product Owners who come from a technical background tend to either work on much larger, complex projects or be the complete opposite, having solved a very particular need in a simple and elegant way.

This is most evident when you look at the history of technical founders. Historically, first-time technical founders tend to have little to no practical experience in owning the build of a real-life product, but have created something that solved an issue they themselves were facing. In doing so, they tend to have taken a very solution-oriented approach but may have missed some of the nuances of making the solution approachable for a larger audience. This is not always the case, of course, but the kind of focus that it often takes to solve a problem is not always beneficial when trying to create something scalable and relevant.

There has also been an influx of designers getting into product ownership. This particular discipline has always been the most interesting to me. Designers of any kind have an intuition and closeness to the user that very few other archetypes can even come close to matching. Being able to leverage that user understanding into creating top-tier requirements is an undeniable advantage. However, designers tend to struggle with the same issue many sales-focused people do, which is the word "no." Sometimes, even when there is an answer that would make the users life a bit easier, the right answer is still "no." There is a fine line between being appropriately compassionate and being so empathetic to the user can that you lose empathy for the people who are required to actually build it.

At the end of the day, the point here is that the only tried and true way to become a good product person is to become a product person. I know that sounds trite, but it's true. Regardless of your role or responsibility in an organization, if you take the initiative to suss out a solvable problem, speculate on how to best solve that problem, do a reasonable but not absurd amount of research into what it would take and that it is worth solving that problem, guess what—you've got the makings of a Product Owner.

While many organizations might look for you to have experience or opinions on process and tooling, the fact is all of that can be easily learned and adapted to through reading and moderate observation. The truth is that a lot of what has become standard practices for Product teams is ripe for improvement. While there is value and learning to be had from the way things have been done, as the things being built change, it makes sense for how we build them to change as well. If anything, coming in with no preconceived notion of HOW one must work to get something done, instead being only mindful of getting the work done, could go a long way in teaching some companies about what truly being Agile means.

The very first role of Product is to be hopelessly and painfully curious.

The second role of Product Leadership is to be fearless in making decisions.

# The Ultimate Product Leadership Guide: Responsibilities and Realities

**5**

As defined by many, CEOs and Product Leaders are responsible for guiding the success of a Product and leading the various necessary teams that are responsible for improving it. The issue with that definition is that is says nothing about WHAT or HOW that gets done.

The very first role of Product is to be hopelessly and painfully curious. If you meet a Product person who rarely uses the word "why" and instead seems to have an answer for everything, they are likely miscast in their role. In order to be successful at building things you need to have an insatiable appetite for understanding WHY people want the thing they are asking for. This is mostly because people ask for something because they believe it is what will solve the problem they have, often not understanding what the actual problem is (which we will discuss later). An important distinction here is that "curious" is not and should not be synonymous with "indecisive," which brings us to our next point.

The second role of Product Leadership is to be fearless in making decisions. In the words of Stan Lee, "With great power comes great responsibility." If you are properly positioned in your organization and have genuine authority to make the right decisions on behalf of the product, then you have to make decisions. The truth is, you will likely never truly know ahead of time what is right and what is wrong. The next truth is, you are going to be wrong sometimes. But the fundamental and explicit job of Product is to give each option its day in court, run it down as far as is appropriate, and pull the trigger on what makes the most sense. Doing this and owning the decisions you make is paramount to having teams who respect you, executives who trust you, and customers who appreciate you. As Ernest Hemingway said, "The first draft of anything is shit." If you are aiming to release the perfect product, you will, and it will be too late. Decisive always wins over hesitant in digital.

The final role of Product Leadership, simply put, is to be the first one shot when bullets start to fly. By being the owner and definer of the object being created, you stand in the way of all incoming fire, doing everything you can to find signals through the noise.

From a business standpoint, product development can very quickly become product prevention if either salespeople or users hear the word "no" too often. Whether you are dealing with salespeople, consumers, or even engineering customers, it is your job to put rigor and concept around the deluge of asks that you are sure to face. And a large part of the job, unfortunate as it may be, is to say "no." What the best product people I have worked with do, and what I have tried to train my brain to, is move from "no" to "not yet" whenever possible. But even in doing so, you need to keep in mind that one of the main tenets of successfully managing products is properly setting expectations.

From a development standpoint, you are a constant nuisance of timelines that are too tight, features or requests that are unrealistic, and potentially "boring" or uninteresting needs that your team would rather not bother with. Even the best of Product people is all but guaranteed to eventually annoy their development team at some point.

So, in essence, Product's role is to volunteer as tribute in the Hunger Games that is the business world, constantly letting down one side or the other in an effort to deliver something that is close enough to what the business needs while being interesting enough that development will build it. True masters of the craft find a way to convince each side they are winning, and in the rarest of instances can design a product where that is actually the case. But inherently there is a give and take to the role. You are serving ALL masters at once, and as it is in life, there is a balance that requires compromise.

Once you have defined a clear ask and have started to build it, it is your job to ensure that you stay the course. The words "Feature Creep" have kept many a Product Owner up at night. Feature Creep might be an alien term to many, but it is one every Product Owner either is or will be very familiar with. The best example is hosting a dinner party with your friends. It starts out simple: you, as the host, will handle making a turkey and mashed potatoes and you then assign everyone else a responsibility—drinks, sides, desserts. But after you have done so, you start to think of things you forgot. "Shit, no one is bringing gravy. I'm making the turkey, so I'll make the gravy." Then another. And another. And suddenly your super easy "throw the bird in the oven and wait" has turned into a laundry list of tasks and a genuine feeling of panic and dread about this thing you were so excited for originally. The same thing occurs in building products. As you go down the path, it is not only possible but likely that things will change. You will need to adapt to things you cannot do as you assumed, including things you either missed or could not have planned for, and remove things that are either not working or would complicate the end product.

In more traditional, physical product development, it is easier to see if the vision is being executed. Take an architect, for example. While they need to have a thorough understanding of calculus and the materials used to build their vision, they could never once swing a hammer and still know with a degree of certainty whether the product was coming together as intended. By using visual cues and doing walk-throughs, an architect can clearly assess progress and make adjustments if necessary. Architects collaborate with General Contractors to do the physical work and complete the project on time and under budget.

Building digital products follows a similar path. However, as there is no physical walk-through to be done; a Product Owner is left with multiple paths to successfully track the development of their product.

**Product's role is to volunteer as tribute in the Hunger Games that is the business world.**

This is not about how to 'manage people and make friends.' This is squarely about your ability to be self-effacing and position yourself amongst your team in a way that gets their buy-in and respect.

# Visionary or Executor: Shaping Your Product Leadership Identity

**6**

I f you have any misconceptions about who you are or what you know as a Product Leader, you are in for a tough go of it. As we just discussed, you're taking bullets from all angles. In order to do that successfully, you need to be steadfast in your role and leadership style. This is not about how to "manage people and make friends." This is squarely about your ability to be self-effacing and position yourself amongst your team in a way that gets their buy-in and respect and helps clearly define what each person's role will need to be in order to succeed.

Let's continue with our architect metaphor. There are three paths I have identified in my time in the digital world. As with all things, there are advantages and disadvantages to each. These are by no means exhaustive, but as a baseline, they cover the main angles you can take when interacting with the teams you will need to work with in the digital world—especially Engineering. So if you were an architect yourself, you could choose to be one of the following three types:

I.  A general contractor and architect all in one. In the digital world Product folks are becoming more and more fluent in the languages of code they build in. Doing so allows you to not only be a part of the original architecture conversations but also to "spot-check" progress and see how things are coming along. These folks are the true Renaissance Men and Women of the digital age.

II. A student and admirer of general contracting, or what I frequently refer to as "knowing enough to be dangerous." Having a passing understanding of the high level of how the products you define are built but not being so fluent that you are actively swinging a hammer yourself. This requires a strong trust in your Engineering and QA teams. Let's call these folks Sufficiently Aware.

III. Be Deliberately Ignorant—by intentionally focusing solely on the product itself, you relinquish all development decisions to the professionals and "let Jesus take the wheel." This requires blind faith in the team you have around you.

## BEYOND SPECIALIZATION: THE RISE OF THE RENAISSANCE LEADER

Being a general contractor, you are extremely appealing to many. In essence, you are all you need to complete the product you desire to build, but may let others stand in simply as an accelerant to success.

Being an Engineer yourself does, without question, set you up for success. Understanding the minutiae of the build and being able to go both wide and deep in conversations around the best way to build your product can be invaluable. It is also helpful in staffing and recruiting if you can speak the language of the people you are reliant on for delivery. While Engineers can get a bad rap for communication skills, very often I find that they are more than willing to communicate, but might want to do so differently. Inherently they are problem solvers, and if you can speak to them in a way that ignites their passion for problem-solving, you can find yourself in rarified air.

There are downsides to this approach, however. The truth is that, as rapidly as the development world changes in our times, it is damn near a full-time job to keep up with new and updated languages, best practices, and even the subtlety of style in code. So, if you are truly to be able to keep up with the teams you collaborate with you need to, well, keep up. This can be an enormous tax on your time, as well as potentially take you away from the things that very team is relying on you to keep up with.

The other glaring downside is ownership. A large part of any collaborative process is trusting the people who are assigned to a particular aspect of that project. If you are competent enough to be involved and you own the product, you are likely to share your opinion on matters of architecture. In doing so, you might go against or even undermine the very folks you have trusted to build with you. In that case, you run the risk becoming a benevolent dictator, meaning there is no team at all, but instead pairs of hands with little to no true investment in the success of the product beyond doing what was asked of them.

In my experience, I have met very few individuals who could truly straddle both the business and development worlds without becoming unhinged. One of the greatest weapons in a Product Owner's arsenal is the ability to shield Engineering from the chaotic and often unfounded asks from the business side, so representing both of those can sometimes put you at odds.

If you are one of the few who truly can manage both worlds, I recommend you surround yourself with extraordinary support staff (Account Management and Business Development specifically) so that you do not add any additional responsibility to your load.

## BALANCING KNOWLEDGE AND ACTION: THE ART OF BEING SUFFICIENTLY AWARE

In my experience, this is where most Leaders tend to fit. As I mentioned before, being truly tied into the Engineering world is a non-trivial ask of a human being. Being aware of things just enough to understand impact is significantly more reasonable.

The benefits of being Sufficiently Aware may seem somewhat self-evident after reading the downsides of being a Renaissance Leader, but they are worth calling out all the same.

First and foremost, being Sufficiently Aware allows you to be singularly focused on the task at hand. Ultimately your goal is to deliver something meaningful to the end user, and the further you remove yourself from that, the worse off you will be. Being aware of the decisions that are being made, knowing enough to ask the right questions to ensure that your team has asked themselves those questions, and then trusting the judgment of the people designated to make them is a lovely place to operate from.

Another advantage to this approach is the human side. When working to deliver something of value that requires multiple people, you would be wise to account for the ego and emotions of those contributing. Think back to a group project you did in school. There is this innate false sense that whoever presented the project OWNED the project. Delivering products with adults is no different. Often many teams feel that they are only acknowledged when things are wrong or dates are missed, but that Product gets to stand up and present when the mission is accomplished to the jubilation of the larger group. We as humans want to be important and want to be heard. Being only Sufficiently Aware means that you cannot, under any circumstance, stand up there alone (unless you're a terrible person—don't be a terrible person), which can give a sense of ownership and meaning to your team.

This is not a silver bullet, and requires a significant amount of restraint and humility. Knowing enough to be dangerous makes you just that—dangerous. The fine line between saving your team by knowing enough and burying your team by not knowing enough is a very thin one.

I myself resemble this kind of Product Owner. I can "hang" to a certain extent in most technical and architectural calls, but there is a very clear point at which I am over my depth. This can become dangerous for a number of reasons:

- You don't know what you don't know. The fact of the digital world is that as amazing as it is and as fast as it has grown, there are still very hard and fast technical limitations. So, when scoping a product, not knowing where those limits lie is an enormous liability. Assuming something can be done because you have "seen something like it" is a death trap that can and will cause your Engineers to hate the very ground you walk on.

- Integrations are harder than you think—we non-technical people of the world tend to believe there is some magic language that all data conforms to so that when we need it—POOF—there it is. Unfortunately, that is so far from the actual truth it might surprise you. I have seen the exact same system have such divergent outputs it would make your mind melt. When a requirement of "we need to be able to access" or "we need to ingest" comes up, your instinct might very well be to say "absolutely" or "how hard could it be." Don't. It can be beyond your wildest dreams hard.

- Form factor matters A LOT. While many of us live in the wonderful world where Apps and Websites live in perfect harmony and are just carbon copies of one another, they are not. The fact is that from the type of code, the interactions, and basically everything else, the form factor makes an enormous difference, and each requires special attention and thoughtfulness. There is no silver bullet here, but don't take my word for it, go use Facebook on mobile web . . .

This level of awareness requires you to trust the team around you to be competent and diligent while allowing yourself to focus on the big picture. It requires you to be in a constant state of listening and learning so that you are better informed the next time decisions need to be made that are presently outside of your depth. And most importantly, it requires you to know when to keep your opinions to yourself and simply respond with, "Let me get back to you." If you can follow that simple principle, this path can work.

## THE POWER OF SELECTIVE IGNORANCE IN LEADERSHIP

This kind of Product work is a dream for many who first hear of it—the ability to have truly singular focus, caring only about the endgame and not worrying about the details of how it happens.

If you are reading this and don't get why this would be amazing, I don't know if I can help you. If you are reading this and you have operated under the assumption that this is truly what all Product jobs are like, you have either not had many, or you, my friend, have hit the job lottery.

The fact is that even in very large organizations that tend to believe in hyper-focused precision instrumentation of roles, this is a hard thing to accomplish. Explicitly drawing lines where you do and don't interact in something as fluid as Product is difficult, to put it mildly.

When this is accomplished, the upside is glaring. With no concerns as to how things are delivered or the impact of delivery on other products or even the greater good, the proverbial "sandbox" most people work in looks more like a Zen sand garden. You are free to make requests with reckless abandon and simply refine the product as the answers come in.

This also allows for the creation of user stories and needs that otherwise might not ever make it to paper, as in both other scenarios they would likely be shut down before even being said out loud.

The downside to this is unfortunately simple—it's not very realistic. Outside of innovation practices or think tanks, building a product usually requires you to start from a basis of truth and defined need, not from a blue-sky state.

It is possible to create an environment where this thrives, however. It is most likely to exist for products within a product, where the walls of that product are well defined and immovable. In those cases, you can have laser-focused product people bouncing wildly off those walls and relying exclusively on the collaborating teams to course-correct where necessary. So, this is not never-never land, but it is not something you see outside of very large, very polished, very defined organizations.

On a personal note—being Deliberately Ignorant inside a box isn't as much fun as being universally Deliberately Ignorant, so keep that in mind if and when these roles are made available to you.

This kind of Product work is a dream
for many who first hear of it—

the ability to have
truly singular focus

caring only about the endgame and not
worrying about the details of how it happens

# The absolute truth of your job as a Product Owner is that the only master you truly serve is your end user.

# User-Centric or Bust: The Unspoken Rule of Product Success

I n 1986, Donald A. Norman, a professor at the University of California, San Diego, coined the term "User-Centered Design" in *User-Centered System Design: New Perspectives on Human-Computer Interaction*, a book he released in 1986. But it wasn't until he wrote *The Design of Everyday Things*, which he released in 1988, that the term really took hold.

The concept is a rather simple one—follow a framework where you define the goals, users, use cases, and workflow of a product; pay close attention to each of those swim lanes prior to, during and after the build; test them extensively in as close to a real-world environment as possible; repeat.

The breakthrough of the above is one that still astonishes me to this day—namely, that to follow Norman's practice, you as the product creator and owner had to surrender that your user might know what they want better than you do.

There are plenty of examples that people reference constantly as to why this might not always be the case. The most famous one comes from Henry Ford, who said, "If I asked people what they wanted, they would have said faster horses." But the misnomer here is that there is a huge difference between invention and innovation. The vast majority of products being built are improvements on existing technology or the marriage of different technologies to accomplish a goal. So rarely are you building something so truly new that your users are completely ill-equipped to handle it and therefore completely useless in helping you make decisions for the product. And even then, given the time we exist in today, inclusion of users early and often has proven time and again to be more useful than not.

The absolute truth of your job as a Product Owner is that the only master you truly serve is your end user. Everyone else whom you need to align and coordinate closely with is also serving the user. So, at any point that you find yourself not feeling the need to check in with the people who will actually engage with your product, take a HARD pause and reset.

I very often hear people say that there is such thing as too much user feedback, that you can get to a point where there is so much data that it becomes nearly impossible to distinguish what is meaningful and what is not. If that is the case, that is 100 percent a "you" problem.

The fear of "paralysis by analysis" in user-generated feedback only exists if you allow it to. Data is always "garbage in, garbage out," and if you are getting "garbage in," that means you did not take the time to think through the tasks or question you asked of your test users. You need to spend time thinking about the product itself, define the different actors who will engage with the product, and outline

WHAT the product means to them. If you have four different actors and are asking them the same questions, you have already failed.

User testing and feedback gathering needs to be just as thoughtful as the design of the product itself. Failing to take this part of the craft seriously will all but guarantee failure with every portion that follows.

When you receive feedback, you need to take the time to truly interpret the data. If you set the questions and tasks up clearly, this should not be a monumental task, but it does require you to comb through the responses in great detail to extract what is meaningful. This goes back to the need for Product to be decisive. The fact is that with VERY few exceptions you will never fulfill 100 percent of the needs of your user, ever. But being able to weigh them through observation and feedback is at the absolute core of the role.

It's an existential crisis of sorts, but over time you learn that it is in fact not your product, it's theirs. You are simply the vehicle that delivers it to them. People today are more than happy to give feedback (see: Yelp), so ask them honestly and often, and don't be too proud to be wrong. It will serve you, and them, in immeasurable ways. And if you find yourself in a room where the discussion is about worrying less about your users and trusting your gut/team/etc., get the hell out of that room. No matter what product you are creating, you should never need to be reminded to be looking at your work through your users' eyes. Ever.

The race to be first to market is a trivial and non-meaningful one. The 'exit' for MySpace to Murdoch was super meaningful, but if your intention is to truly build the best product, being measured and right is better than being first.

# Staying on Course: How Not to 'Jump the Shark' in Product Strategy

**8**

I n this incredible digital age in which we reside, there is no shortage of shiny objects. For as long as I have been in business, every six months to a year there has been a new technology that was going to change everything. And, as we as humans tend to do, we gravitate toward the new thing as though our very existence depends on it. From 5G to Augmented and Virtual Reality to electric cars to the blockchain (cryptocurrency), the digital generation has turned us from fearful of change to being ravenous for it. And that bleeds into business as well.

The need to develop on new platforms and to be cutting edge has driven investment and business plans in unquantifiable ways. The volume of start-ups that come into existence within the first two months of a new hot topic is staggering. But why? Is it truly possible that something so completely new can have that kind of positive impact so quickly? The answer is almost always no.

As a product person, your role is not to know MORE than your users, but to understand what you are building and how it fits into your users' lives. A big part of this, especially in the digital age, is understanding if the technology you are using is actually ready for human consumption. The fact is that over time all these platforms or languages or technologies could have genuine practical application, but it is incumbent on you as the Product Owner to answer a very important question: "Is this actually good or is just good enough?" There are a multitude of examples of technologies that have been ruined or have grown significantly slower than they should have based on being rushed into market to solve the "shiny object" need. My two recent favorites follow:

## VOICE AND VIRTUAL ASSISTANTS

Have you ever heard of Cortana? I bet a lot of you haven't. What about Alexa or Siri? Have you ever tried to use either of those virtual assistants with your voice? How did that go for you? If you had to peg a percent of time that it works exactly as you intended, is it fifty percent? Seventy-five percent? More?

Voice is the most natural method with which modern humans communicate, so much so that we often speak to ourselves to get to a resolution. But the impetus behind using voice is the speed, ease, and accuracy with which we can access information. Not to mention the added benefit of being able to multi-task with the devices that are permanently glued to our hands. So, when putting together the concept of all the amazing things Virtual Assistants could do, the list could be nearly endless. But where user-centric design should have played a larger role was in seeing how the technology ACTUALLY worked in real life environments, not how it was intended to work.

Siri was released in February of 2010 as a standalone application in the Apple store and was subsequently acquired by Apple two months later. In October of 2011, it was integrated in the iPhone 4's release as a standard feature. At the time, technology magazines and blogs universally praised Apple for innovation of the highest magnitude. But in November of 2014, Amazon released Alexa. Alexa had parity with Siri in much of its functionality, but it shone a light on the issues Siri had been plagued with that had hurt its adoption.

The voice recognition itself was not great. From the software to the microphones used, you needed near perfect speech patterns and a truly quiet environment to be able to communicate with the device. The even larger issue was that, as it was part of the Apple ecosystem, it could only interact with other Apple platforms, and given how specific Apple is in what they do and do not make, this meant it was highly limited in usefulness right out of the gate. This robbed the Virtual Assistant of much of its promise, as it was now not a stand-alone product receiving the kind of attention it deserved but a feature in a much larger product. This left Siri being more "cute" than functional, which in turn had a tremendous effect on the adoption of voice in general, as the technology proved to be only barely useful to most users.

When Alexa was released, it was built and marketed as a hyper-focused product with a clear goal. Even the name, "Alexa," was chosen because of the hard "X" sound, to ensure it would "wake up" when called. This kind of attention to detail, understanding what challenges the user would face, is not being SMARTER than your user, but being empathetic and understanding of them.

Where we stand today with voice is that the Voice technology is not actually holding back the platforms anymore, the immaturity of the Artificial Intelligence that drives Voice is. Virtual Assistants rely on AI to be able to make distinctions prior to making their decisions in how they respond to you. Today, AI can handle clear, linear requests with decent accuracy, but if you include multi-faceted questions or the nuance in human language, AI fails. These are the kinds of questions successful Product Owners should be asking of the technology they are building against to ensure users are realizing actual benefit. And, once again, the answer can be "not yet."

This is one of my favorite use cases, as it is something that ONLY could be tested with humans. Unlike applications that require physical interaction or even data streams where you can automate much of testing, missing on something where you inherently HAVE to test with your users is unforgivable.

## QR CODES

QR codes, or quick response codes, were first introduced for the automotive industry in Japan in 1994 by the company Dense Wave. They created these scannable, two-dimensional barcodes to track vehicles during the manufacturing process. It was a quick solution to be able to easily track how a product was making its way through assembly.

It was clear early on that QR codes had significantly more uses than just what they were built for. But for the purposes of understanding user-centric design, I want to focus on the multiple attempts to use them in the Advertising Industry over the years.

In a vacuum, putting together a case for why QR codes would be a brilliant way to engage with your consumers via their mobile devices is not a leap in any way, shape, or form. People are carrying a device around with them that has access to the internet and has a camera which could, in theory, activate against QR codes, allowing companies to engage directly with consumers. You could place QR codes on street corners, in stores, in restaurants, on public transportation, and allow your potential customers to immediately engage with your brand. But there have been huge, glaring issues that were either completely ignored or simply underestimated that have stood in the way of the success of a completely feasible technology.

The first and largest issues was meaningful connectivity. Having access to the internet and access to a camera was the absolute baseline for this to come together. When originally released, not all phone cameras knew how to read a QR code and launch something. It required a piece of software, meaning you needed to include this as core functionality or have this built into an application. So now, it's not as simple as seeing a QR code in the wild. It requires the user to have their phone, potentially open an application that they already have (or need to get), give that application access to their camera (which, depending on the application, might make NO sense beyond this single use case), scan the QR code, and THEN get to the place you intend them to. That is a non-trivial user journey.

The other huge misstep in understanding this product from the user's standpoint was education. QR codes are only meaningful if the user knows what the hell they are. It would require meaningful scale and consistency for a standard user to even understand what they are supposed to do in order to leverage this kind of technology. In focus groups or controlled user testing, you are handing people a phone in a controlled environment where they have assistance and guidance as to what the action is.

In both of these examples, had anyone taken a step back and asked better questions about whether "we really are in a place to make this work for users," both these technologies might be further along, or have better adoption.

The argument here is what I refer to as the "Apple Headphone and AirPods Dilemma." If you are an iPhone user, when Apple first released iPhones without headphone jacks you were likely less than thrilled. This was of course quickly followed by the subsequent release of AirPods, which had all the little Apple fans in line, rushing to get this marvel of long-existing technologies and, in turn, my brain almost exploded. Why, you ask? Because, as an audiophile, I hate Bluetooth headphones for listening to high bitrate music. Why is that, you ask? Because they suck. But Apple, in a way that very few companies are able to do, can push people into Bluetooth headsets and, some would argue, force Bluetooth technology to get better because of it. But I would argue that, in a time where we are constantly looking for improvement in existing technologies, I cannot think of a single example where we have forced a technology to get better quickly.

Now, between when I originally wrote this book and the time you are reading it, a global pandemic has served as the vehicle to make QR codes really shine. The functionality is now inherently baked into all phone cameras, and most people have figured out how to leverage them, which, in my opinion, is awesome. But I hope that this is a one-off way to leverage existing technology, as I think we would all prefer to avoid pandemics in the future.

## ARTIFICIAL INTELLIGENCE

It's happening. And it can either happen to you or for you. Artificial Intelligence (AI) is here and it is here to stay. But before you go "All in" on AI, be thoughtful about what you are trying to solve with it.

I could (and might) write an entire book on AI in the workforce. For this conversation, let's focus very specifically on what it is GREAT at.

AI as an accelerant to productivity and creativity is amazing. As a thought starter, a story boarder, a work checker, it's uses are nearly limitless. But even as the Co-Founder of a start-up in the space, be careful.

The truth is there is a LOT it cannot do yet. And just like the two earlier examples, giving people access to something that has ALL the promise but is not perfected can be dangerous. It can be dangerous for the people using it, it can be dangerous for the companies deploying it, and long term it can be dangerous for the technology itself.

The best guidance I can offer is to take small steps into AI. Embrace the "Human in the Loop" method to start, where you don't let it be responsible for any one thing but allow it to be an assistant of sorts to certain roles. Make sure you are deploying the things that are further along (Chat, as an example) so that people see its usefulness in ways where it has been well tested.

The most important part of embracing the "Human in the Loop" attitude, however, is the "Human" part. Remember that there is a lot of fear and unknowns in AI still, and in some instances for good reason. So starting a tornado of activity around "automation" leveraging the technology is going to be a signal to your employees. What kind of signal will be based entirely on how you frame the work. Is AI a part of your roadmap to help your EMPLOYEES be more efficient, more creative and get more time, or is it for your bottom line? The answer to that question matters, and not just to the people you employ. It should matter to you. How you approach this kind of industry altering technology from the beginning sets the stage for what kind of company you will be as the technology grows.

Reach out to experts, do your own research and form some early opinions you can test without setting the building on fire. This is not a small change, it's a seismic one. Be mindful.

# Is this actually good or is it just good enough?

There are a multitude of examples of technologies that have been ruined or have grown significantly slower than they should have based on being rushed into market.

Successful product people need to be like that toddler—relentlessly curious and unsatisfied with the answer until they either pass out or are genuinely satisfied.

# Provoking Progress: Challenging Teams for Better Results

**9**

W hat do toddlers and good product people have in common? The incessant need to ask "why?" As anyone who has ever spent any meaningful time with a toddler knows, "why" is a black hole from which you cannot escape. It will start with something trivial, like cereal. And somehow, twenty minutes later you will be poorly explaining how atoms work while scanning the room for absolutely anything to "accidentally" cut yourself on so you can walk away with only a small amount of guilt and a solid excuse.

Successful product people need to be like that toddler—relentlessly curious and unsatisfied with the answer until they either pass out or are genuinely satisfied. Part of the plight of Product is that you don't know all the answers and need to rely on the expertise of others to get the full picture. But it is 100 percent your job to not do so on blind faith. You need to sharpen your ability to pester, annoy, and badger your way into the heads of your collaborators until you are comfortable that every scenario has been covered.

## EMPOWERING ENGINEERS

Getting in the heads of Engineers is a dangerous game. It can be dark in there. But what really drives the kind of questions you ask and how you ask them is based entirely on the discussion from earlier—namely, what kind of Product person do you want to be?

If you are a Renaissance leader, this is truly a test of your patience and your resolve. The goal is to push your Engineers to do the hard work of truly looking into all the potential options for a build. This can include what language something is written in, what platforms are used for accessing and storing data, and any number of non-trivial decisions. In the case of building products within an ecosystem or within an existing organization, many of those decisions may be pre-determined based on vendors or architecture that is already in place. But in the early days, if as nothing other than a thought experiment, it is worth sitting down with your Engineering team and asking the question, "If you could do this exactly as you wanted with no limitations, how would you do it and why?"

As a Renaissance leader the key is to keep your opinions to yourself. Unless you are truly the lead Engineer and Product Owner (or as some might call it, the CEO of a small startup), while being inquisitive and pushing is fair, you need to allow the team to be heard and acknowledged, not push them in the direction you would go based on your engineering inclinations.

For the Sufficiently Aware and the Deliberately Ignorant Product folks, this conversation takes an entirely different form, as you likely wouldn't know if you were being lied to. But the good news is you can find out. How, you wonder? Two things you need to do: Ask for details around all the decisions being made by the team, even if you aren't 100 percent confident the words they say will mean all that much to you. And then, when they answer, ask them why. If the answer is anything that resembles "Because I said so" or "That's how we do it," demand more detail. If they refuse, threaten them like you would a doctor, telling them you will seek a second opinion if you don't get the appropriate amount of insight. If you don't have an internal option for a second opinion, go find one. While this might sound extreme, and the goal is not be adversarial, I promise you that most Engineers will hold you to a similar standard when you ask for something, so be confident and empowered to require the level of detail you require to feel diligence has been performed, or else.

Taking Action – Be self-aware and honest. If you don't know something, or if you think you might know something but are not 100 percent sure, shut your mouth and go ask. No Engineer wants to build something that doesn't work or isn't great, so give them the chance to participate early and often and take their feedback to heart. If you have ever had a group project where you didn't have full visibility over what was being done and the end result made you sick to have your name attached to it, remember that feeling and refuse to allow your Engineers to feel it. Also, regardless of your acumen, do your best to understand the day in and day out challenges of your team. You can be clueless but empathetic, and it will go a long way in winning hearts and minds.

## SUPPORTING SALES

Now depending on the product, there might not be a "business" function you need to interact with. But more often than not, there is some arm you will need to answer to that is concerned with either the sale or profitability of whatever you are building. And having open, consistent dialogue with that group can go a long way.

Having come from sales, I have been in the world of product and technology being a black box. The analogy I most often use is that of a restaurant—there is the front of the house and the back of the house. The front of the house is polished, composed, and beautiful. The back of the house is chaos, frantically working to make the front of the house look good. At the end of service, the front of the house all go out together and talk about how the back of the house was slow that night, needlessly grouchy, and are just impossible to work with. That same night, the back of the house goes out to lament about how they were set up for failure from the very start. Too many reservations, no one pushing easier dishes, and can that many people seriously be allergic to things???

When this works well in restaurants, it works well because of communication and planning. Building digital products is exactly the same. The business, or the "front of the house," is the voice of the customers. They are closer to the customer than anyone else, so they do have legitimate insight that can help shape your product. But it's important to remain aware of their motives. While it goes against the idea of "consultative selling," unless incentivized to do the "right" thing and not the "profitable" thing, business folks can push for bigger and better (read that as "more expensive") even if it's not truly what their clients need.

All the same, allowing their voices to be heard and collecting as much data from them as possible is not only worthwhile but required to maintain an inclusive atmosphere, which, while it may sound soft and very millennial-like, is important to your success.

Taking Action – Don't be sales prevention. Engage with the people who are the face to your product and truly listen to what they say. Don't bullshit them to make them go away; if you can't do something or believe you shouldn't, say it to their face and explain why. They might not love you for it, but in the long run, having a chance to make their case instead of being appeased is what they are after.

## NAVIGATING FINANCE

Unlike the externally focused folks, this is more about how you handle the "money guy/gals" in your organization. As previously mentioned, you either are or should regard yourself as the CEO of the product you are creating, so understanding the cost to build, release, maintain, and support is 100 percent in your purview. It is also something that very few people can do alone.

The key to successfully managing the finances of a product forces me to use a phrase I hate. However in this instance it is 100 percent accurate—"You can't manage what you can't measure." Truly tracking a product's cost to build/maintain is more an exercise of will than anything else. Be it with time-tracking tools (your Engineering team will hate your very existence) or through the not-so-clever use of spreadsheets and level of effort (LOE) estimates, staying on top of who is doing what and when, while a painful and often laborious process, is a necessary one.

Personally, I have never been one to track an individual's times. The truth is that everyone's time is not created equal, and it will save you a lot of headache in your product life if you come to terms with that sooner rather than later. But understanding how long it takes to complete certain aspects of building your product, the different actors involved in putting it together, and being able to explain—in your native tongue and without the use of tech jargon—to a CFO object why it took the time it did and how efficient or inefficient a particular process was is very much your job.

Another personal note around LOE estimates is that no one works 100 percent of the time on any one thing. They don't. Observe your own behavior. You might literally be on Instagram as you read this. So, in the planning phase, if you get an estimate of eighty hours from your team, it's not one person for two weeks. It's one person for closer to three weeks, because you work with humans, not robots.

The main reason you need to stay on top of resources goes beyond the obvious. A huge benefit of digital products is that you can adjust them while they are in the wild. Being able to do that will require you to have the resources to make those changes. Getting the resources to be able to make the changes you want to require you to have the trust of whoever controls the purse strings in your organization. The easiest and most effective way to gain that trust is to accurately report what is happening as it happens. This is not the fun part of the job, and it can easily turn into "tattletale" culture, where it feels like product is out to spy on the teams and report back the bad actors. But that's entirely based on how you set expectations and how you handle them.

The best product people I have seen work with Finance are constantly advocates for their teams, easily explaining that if dates or features are slipping, it is not because the team is not working but because the ask was too great, or the team is under-resourced. Being able to eloquently and concisely provide that feedback to the finance team will go a long way in gaining the trust and admiration of the teams you work with.

Taking Action — Do. The. Work. It's that simple. Good Finance people need to know what they need to know, and if you can deliver that consistently and in a format that they can digest, they will likely leave you alone. So, establish the cadence and output early, stick to it, and be on your merry way. Nothing good gets built without these folks in your corner, so get them in your corner.

## UTILIZING PROJECT MANAGEMENT

One thing that needs to be made clear right out of the gate is the difference between Project and Product Management. In its simplest terms, Product Owners are the CEOs of a particular product, driving the requirements, development, and deployment of that product. Project Managers are in charge of executing against a single task or a group of tasks in a clearly specified timeline as part of a larger project.

The function of Project Management is one I have struggled with for years. On one hand, it would make sense that breaking large products or projects into smaller, tangible objects and having people drive those portions to completion makes perfect sense. On the other hand, depending on the size of the product and the size of the team, the role can start to feel redundant and, if anything, create more work than needed.

As a rule of thumb, if the entire team can sit in a standard-size conference room without busting at the seams or being elbow to elbow, I don't believe Project Managers should be involved. This, of course, operates under the presupposition that you have capable and communicative Product and Engineering resources who can act without adult supervision.

Where Project Management does make sense to me is when a single team is handling multiple projects or when the size and scale of the product is such that it requires either multiple resource groups or multiple resource types to work in parallel. But the goal of a Project Manager should be to keep the lines of communications open and assess/report on liability and potential issues TO the core Product team. The function itself is one of visibility and timekeeping, not one of creation or decisioning.

Great Product people with great Engineering will tend to project-manage themselves. If you can fit everyone in one conference room and still require a person/people to coordinate, you have a communication issue, not a missing actor.

In my experience, Project Managers tend to be very timeline- and date-driven. This can be useful at multiple stages of building a product.

Planning the build of any product is always a challenge. In the digital world, properly scoping the level of effort (LOE) and time to build is easily one of the least favorite tasks of most Engineers. If you have

Project Managers who can lead this process, get in their kitchen to figure out how confident they are about the timelines. Push them to tell you how much padding they've built in to protect themselves if they underestimated effort.

Once the build has begun, leverage their proximity to the Engineering team to stay updated, but also keep asking them where there seems to be exposure. Engineers can get into "problem-solving" mode and start to lose sight of the big picture. If you have a Project Manager implemented with the team, constantly converse with them about the big picture, forcing them to ask the question you might not be able to.

I stand behind my conference room concept, but a smart person on your side is a smart person on your side. Ignoring a function that is implemented in your organization will get you nowhere, so search for ways to communicate with your Project Manager that gets you data or insight you otherwise wouldn't get.

Taking Action – Identify where you are most exposed on missing detail or potential disruption and insert talented people there to mitigate. Make sure you communicate openly and often but remained focused exclusively on delivering the right thing. Timing is a part of life, and properly using resources is a must, but don't let either dictate the course of what you are building. Project Management that is clear on and working toward your north star is invaluable. Project Management that creates loads of meaningless busywork is nothing but a distraction. It's on you to ensure it's the former.

# CHAMPIONING PARTNERSHIP / BUSINESS DEVELOPMENT

The term "Business Development" is now, and has for years been, one of the most confusing terms in the digital world. I genuinely have no idea what it is has come to mean. I have heard it used in the context of creating new business (more traditionally known as "sales"), I have used it to very specifically mean Mergers and Acquisitions (M&A), and I have heard it refer to a person whose role it is to form partnerships and integrations. For the purposes of this book, let's assume it's the latter.

In the digital world, there are very few products that do not require you to have some kind of partnership. Whether it be using Facebook or Google to sign in to an online application, working with a third party to provide a certain data set (think Nielsen for ratings data in the media space), or even working with a payment processing company for your e-commerce offering, partnerships are rarely not a consideration. However, often I find they are not given the time or attention they deserve.

The first thing to look at with potential partners is the most obvious: does this make my product easier to engage or interact with for my user? If there is any question, push back with full force until the case for why you should move forward is beyond reproach. A default answer I hear often from Biz Dev co-workers is "Our competition has it." Outside of clearly necessary partnerships, as mentioned above, don't assume that their involvement with your competition equates to them being must-haves for your own product. You never know the impetus one company might have to work with another.

I often find that reasons such as mutual investors, board member connections, or even something as trivial as individual connections to an old buddy can spawn "partnerships," so take the investigation of true benefit seriously and force your collaborators to do the work.

Always be weary of anyone using the term "seamless integrations." The issue with the way partnerships are handled in much of the digital world is that you have two people, charged with getting partners, driving the conversation. Their instinct to be agreeable and get the ball moving—while admirable—is not ideal. If you have been presented a clear use case that truly has a positive impact on your product, get your technical team involved early and insist that your potential partner does as well. The number of deals I have seen fall through or become icebergs (something that looks small on the surface but with a tremendous amount underneath) because of lack of early technical diligence might surprise you.

There is a lack of partnership in the digital world often based on company ego and a desire to do everything on one's own. In that way, digital is immature and needs to get over itself. Airlines don't make planes, hotels put Starbucks in their lobbies because they don't know how to run a coffee business, and automotive companies don't mine gas. We would all be wise to learn from industries much older than ours to remain focused on what we do best, but more about that later.

Taking Action – Understand what the role of Business Development truly is for your product and work with them to set them up for success. Give them as much information as possible, leaving little to the imagination, so they are blunt objects in the field looking to do right by the product. If they are on the wrong course, get involved and help them get back on track. And if they are discovering new and interesting courses to explore, listen actively and engage. Similar to sales, turning "no" into "not yet," or at the very least providing good answers to a "no," will only help you—and in turn them—in the long run.

## EMBRACING USERS

Users are the most delicate and most important of your collaborators. Whereas I am a firm believer in genuinely annoying your other counterparts until you are satiated with the information required, users cannot be annoyed. Or, at the very least, they can't know that they are being annoyed.

In the pre-release world, your "users" are most likely focus groups or alpha/beta users. These folks can be lightly pestered for feedback as long as you set the stage for what the engagement will be well in advance of them getting their hands on whatever you are building. The key is to be concise and clear in both your initial direction and follow up. People have a threshold for communication. Think about the worst two kinds of people you text with—there is the paragraph writer and the bullet texter. One writes epic novels in a single shot that when you open them make you say, out loud, "You have got to be kidding me." The other hits you with thirty texts in a row, some with half-thoughts, some fully formed, some seemingly out of place entirely. Depending on your personality, one might be preferable to the other, but generally speaking, neither are great. Your users are just like you. They want to be spoken to when appropriate, and with substance. So even if you set the expectation that there will be a heavy flow of communication, be thoughtful and deliberate all the same.

Once your product is in the wild, continuing to get feedback from your users should be a non-negotiable. There are very few "set it and forget it" products in the digital world. Things change too frequently and too drastically. How you go about garnering that feedback is more meaningful than you might think.

Have you ever downloaded an app that asks you to rate it every time you open it? Does that make you happy? Are you likely to give meaningful feedback if, after you were asked once, you continually are asked over and over and over again to do the thing you already said you'd pass on? Most apps have taken to using the language "Are you enjoying this app?", prompting you to select yes or no. If yes, they send you to the app store where you are prompted to give a review. If no, they send you to a support ticket email where you can vent and vent, but only to the app owners directly, not to the whole world.

Users are wise to this. Even digital non-natives have lived in the digital world long enough to catch up. You can't just throw "Give us feedback" at people and expect them to give you meaningful answers. Your users are HUMAN. Like all humans, they do better with context.

Here is a list of approaches I have found helpful in garnering meaningful feedback from users:

## ASK THEIR PERMISSION

Just like with everything else in life, consent is key. Far too often, platforms and products presume that users want something. The crackdown on the use of cookies in 2019, where websites have been forced to alert users to the use of cookies and have them opt in, is the perfect example. For too long in the digital world we acted as though we didn't require permission for anything we did. That time has come and gone, and interacting with users now requires you to treat them as though you could be bothered with what they think and feel. So, when approaching users, you need to do so with respect and consent. Basically, don't be a dick about it.

## TELL THEM UP FRONT WHAT'S INVOLVED

Along with consent comes a clear understanding of what is about to go down. As has been long established, showing users where they are on the journey is a tried-and-true practice, and the absolute LEAST you can do (think about progress bars on every online survey you have ever taken). But I would argue that you can go a full step further. Let's stick with the "Are you enjoying this app" concept. Instead of that language, why not be direct and concise and ask explicitly, "Do you have three minutes to tell us what we are doing well and what bums you out?" In that example, you are asking them if they want to engage AND being specific as to what they are in for if they so choose to jump in. Additional context here that was at one time standard, but we have lost completely, is letting them know WHERE this is going to happen. If you are in an application, on a webpage, or even inside data documentation, and engaging is going to take you out of the experience, PLEASE tell them that. Either do so in advance with "If you do want to help us out, you're gonna transport somewhere else, but don't worry, nothing changes here" OR, once they agree to engage give them a second notification, say something similar to the above and reconfirm they want in, like "Awesome! We're gonna send you somewhere else to do that, but nothing changes here. You still good to help?"

## MAKE IT BEYOND EASY

The truth is, when trying to get feedback from users after you have released your product, they are not likely to spend an inordinate amount of time giving you information. So, it's on you to provide them with a path to giving feedback that is simple to understand and simple to execute.

The best way I have found to get meaningful information that you can actually act on is through multiple choice. But let me be clear as to the kind of choices that work. When you receive survey information back that has asked people to rate "On a scale of 1 to 10, how do you feel about _____," you are basically already done for. The scale is subjective, the volume of data you will need to interpret will be unwieldy if you have scale in your feedback loop, and ultimately people tend to phone those in. Be PRESCRIPTIVE in how you write your questions and your answers. Use lines like "No issues for me" or "This brings me great sadness." Be funny, be witty, use real language, and make it approachable. Obviously, you need to tailor the level with which you can include levity and the kind of levity based on your users, but I highly encourage you to try. People like being spoken to as people, as it turns out.

Try to keep it to three to five questions with no more than four answers to choose from, one of those answers being something to the effect of "I don't care about this." Believe it or not, that is one of the most powerful things you will hear from your user base, and finding out can save you more time and energy than you can imagine. Instagram famously deleted the "Following" tab, much to the chagrin of—wait for it—no one. Barely anyone even noticed. It was used sparingly and by very few users, yet made a decent amount of news for Instagram upon its removal. Had they noticed they could have ripped it out earlier, they could have saved themselves some headlines.

What this also means is stay away from essay style answers. Not only is it an enormous headache for you to sift through (even using state-of-the-art machine learning to gather feedback), but the sentiment and context will be lost on you. Reading an essay-style note from a user without understanding how they answered any of the previous questions can lead you to missing their point entirely, no matter how well-asked or well-answered the question was. Getting heartfelt Ayn Rand-style feedback might make the users feel like they are being heard or might make you feel like you are giving them the best opportunity to be heard. However, the fact is that, unless you are aggressively resourced with analysts to comb through, organize, and curate that feedback into meaningful actionable activities, you are more likely to let down users who took the time and potentially don't see the changes.

The biggest lesson here is that in making it easier for the user, you are actually making it easier for you. Simple, concise, digestible. If you can take a hard look at your product in the wild and identify where you know you could be better, and then let your users confirm or deny your suspicions and rank them based on what would make them happy, everyone wins. This requires you to be brutal with what you have already built, not just with the eye test, but digging into the usage data to identify where opportunity lies.

## BE WARY OF INCENTIVIZING

More and more, I see digital products offering some kind of reward or incentive for giving feedback. While I am a huge proponent of the construct of value exchanges in general (it's how we work as humans), this practice can lead to a ton of false or "compromised" data.

Unfortunately, we have built the digital world in such a way people tend to think that if they say nice things, they will get something, but if they are critical or negative, they will not. (Think about the earlier example of pushing happy users to the app store for ratings and less than happy users to a complaint email form.) So just the very concept of giving someone something for engaging in feedback means you already have a meaningful hurdle to overcome. You can use language here to reinforce that your responses have no effect on your incentive, but even just saying that will make some people suspect.

Even if you can get users past the aforementioned issue, you are introducing an additional fail-point into your feedback collection process. There is quite literally nothing you can do to annoy a user more than to promise them something and have it either not happen or take forever to happen. So, thinking through the logistics of how you are going to facilitate the actual giving of the incentive needs to play a role in constructing the incentive itself. If you are an application or a digital platform that has some form of currency (think "lives" in a video game or actual currency in a commerce environment), it can be a bit more straightforward. However, if you are introducing currency for the first time, be very mindful as to whether you have infrastructure in place to actually handle this without it becoming a shit show.

I want to reiterate that I am in no way against this concept, but if you are going to do it, do it in a way that makes it clear why you are doing it and in a way that you can all but guarantee you can follow through on.

## FOLLOW THE F\*\*K UP!

This is, without question, one of my biggest pet peeves. I am fully aware that my optics when engaging with products is different based on my profession, but it's irritates me more so as a human than as someone who works in product.

If someone takes time out of their day, away from their kids, before they write that lingering email, prior to stepping out for lunch, to help you make your product better, follow up with them. The minimum expectation here should be a "Thank you for participating" email, but I would push you to be even smarter than that.

While automating emails is a more than reasonable assertion for something like this, take the time to create more than one. If you ask five questions, you should be able to bucket the answers into at least two different sentiments—"Happy" or "Unhappy." If the responses you received were overwhelmingly on the positive side, thank them for participating and let them know you are thrilled they are enjoying it but that you are going to continue to work to make it better. This might seem like marketing fodder, but I promise you, it's not.

If the response skewed toward "Unhappy," address it. Be apologetic, let them know you are genuinely sorry they are not getting what they want out of your product and that you want to work on it to make it better. Thank them for taking the time to share that they are having a tough time and promise (and mean it) that you don't take their unhappiness lightly.

This moment, by the way, if you are truly brave, is when you set up an email account just for this particular follow-up and allow them to write a long form statement as to the kind of issues they are having. In this cadence, if after they have already been heard and have nothing to gain beyond your product better serving their needs, they are now willing to take the time to write you and explain how they could be better served, they are a power-user of your product, and it is in your best interest to not only read that email but respond! If you think through all the steps just outlined, to still care enough about what you've built that they want to expand on their feelings and misgivings, this person is meaningful to you in a way that no employee, no paid tester, no one else could possibly be. Follow up with this person and take the time to hear them. It will go a long way in how people feel about your company and your product, and an even longer way in how you empathize with and understand your actual users.

Unless the email is them spewing hate or just someone trolling, in which case you should quickly and without hesitation delete it and move on. In my experience, this is rarely the case.

Taking Action — Before you do anything to, for, or with your users, take a full beat to ask yourself, "If it were me, how would I react to this?" That is everything. Remembering that you are a user yourself is how you ensure you don't screw this up. Think about every single interaction with products you have on a daily basis. Think about the ATM. Think about the Starbucks app you used to order your coffee. Think about the gas pump with the TV in it that yelled at you loudly out of nowhere to let you know Doritos were on sale at eight a.m. Think about all of it. Then ask yourself how each of those things made you feel, and what you would say to the person who did that to you. Done? Good. Now think about what you were about to ask of your users again and move forward as you see fit.

# The goal is to push your Engineers to do the hard work of truly looking into all the potential options for a build.

Failure is not
the opposite of
success; it's part
of the process.

# Learning from Loss: How Failures Lead to Wins

## 10

Time and time again, we have seen that being first to market not only does not guarantee success, but often results in the exact opposite. Attached to shiny new objects is also the predisposition in the human condition for "winning" (read as "first to market"). There is a presumption that with being first comes great benefit and competitive edge. That somehow if you are the first to do something, it signifies that you were the best. Just reading that, I would hope it sounds as ridiculous to you as it does to me typing it.

Think of Friendster, MySpace, and Facebook. (If you are reading this and don't know what Friendster or MySpace are, that's the eventual point.) Friendster was founded in March of 2003 as arguably the earliest of the social network sites. It, much like Facebook today, was an internet gathering space for "friends" to share content, calendars, and anything else they could think of. Facebook was founded on February 4 of 2004 and MySpace was founded on August 1 of the same year. Both were also social networks, with MySpace having a focus on music and Facebook being college only.

By 2005, MySpace was the predominant platform by leaps and bounds. This was thanks to being built on ColdFusion (an Adobe platform built for rapid web development) as opposed to JavaServer Pages, which dramatically increased performance and therefore user satisfaction, and the influx of users (thanks to eUniverse's twenty-some-odd million email addresses used to initially populate the platform). Friendster quickly faded, and after turning down $30 million from Google in 2003 (one of the worst beats in Silicon Valley history), it was all but dead in the United States by 2009.

In 2004 and through 2005, Facebook required a .edu email address to participate, leaving much of the world locked out. In that time, MySpace grew its user base, its following, and its stranglehold on the social networking market. In February of 2005, acting MySpace CEO Chris DeWolfe tried to buy Facebook for $75 million, but the now infamous Facebook CEO, Mark Zuckerberg, turned him down. MySpace was purchased in July of 2005 for $580 million by Rupert Murdoch's News Corporation and continued to grow. On August 9 of 2006, MySpace hit its hundred millionth account. For perspective, Facebook had twelve million users to close out 2006.

But on September 26, 2006, all that changed. Facebook opened the doors to anyone thirteen years of age or older with a valid email address. For two years, while MySpace grew its user base but did little to enhance its platform, Facebook was changing dynamically based on user feedback, and including more and more features. They took profiles to another level, included games, and potentially most impactfully built "The Wall," which was a timeline of events associated with each user. So, by garnering feedback, being able to rapidly change without enormous impact, and NOT being first to market, Facebook leaped MySpace in unique visits in mid-2008 and by 2009 had almost double the user base. Today, the first two companies are defunct or shells of their former selves, while the last to market does $53 billion in annual revenue with net income of over $22 billion.

Trust me, it is not my intention to sing the praises of Facebook. But the lesson here is an important one. The race to be first to market is a trivial and non-meaningful one. The "exit" for MySpace to Murdoch was super meaningful, and no one would scoff at that payday, but if your intention is to truly build the best product, being measured and right is better than being first. First is easy, right is significantly more work.

The hardest part in not being first is getting and maintaining buy-in from the team and the organization that getting it right is worth the risk that the "first" product doesn't end up being good enough. While there is never a guarantee, there are steps you can take toward making your case.

The first is to do the market research and document the shit out of it. Even if it is truly a new new product, actually do the research as to how things like it have done. If you can't get the information you need for free, demand to pay for it. In the age in which we currently live, there is data on just about anything you want, but it doesn't always come free. Not getting in front of the market, what it will bear, and what it won't is squarely your responsibility, even if it's not in your job description. If your name is attached to it, this is a must. And while you can always be wrong, not doing so is simply irresponsible.

The other step to take is to stalk the ever-loving shit out of your competition shamelessly. And do so intelligently. Competition is good, and even if they were rushing to market, that does not take away from the fact that people put thought, resources, and time into creating a thing. This is not a plug to steal. It's also not a plug not to. The fact is, if your competition has a laundry list of things you think you should steal, they are already way ahead of you. In this case, you are in real trouble, or you misread the room and they are not really your competition, which means you either don't get your own product or you don't get theirs—both not great. Being honest with yourself if either of those two things are the case is your only choice.

# You don't fail until you stop trying.

The lesson here is not 'use all the tools.' The lesson here is actually learned from the dresser manufacturer: you don't actually require anything more than a **simple solution and patience** to get the job done.

# Tool Mastery: Balancing Utility with Over-Dependence

## 11

S o, you buy a new house and desperately need a new dresser. You have progressed beyond particleboard furniture and want something more substantial, something you can have for a long time. You shop around and finally find one you like. When checking out, your pride gets the better of you and you decide not to have it assembled for you, that you can easily do this yourself. So, you get your dresser home, and to your surprise, there are actually a ton of pieces. The directions are twenty pages long. It says you need two people to build it. And what do you get from the manufacturer to build said dresser? An Allen wrench and a dream. This is why so many comedians have a bit about Ikea and divorce.

What might surprise you, however, is that the lesson here is not "use all the tools." The lesson here is actually learned from the dresser manufacturer.

If you have power tools of all shapes and sizes that clearly would make your life easier and make the job go faster without sacrificing quality, then of course you should use them. But there is beauty in that Allen wrench. The fact is you don't actually require anything more than a simple solution and patience to get the job done. While you are welcome to (and will) curse them when you open the fifteen packets of screws, wooden dowels, and assortment of rubber pieces, then look down at your lone Allen wrench, take a beat, and appreciate the elegance in designing something that could be put together with so little and hold so much.

Your product is that dresser. If you strip back all the things you will be told you need, all the tools and processes and Post-it notes and forms, you can likely build it with very, very little. I have found that often the absolute best product thinking occurs when everything is removed in a room except smart people and a few pads of paper and pens.

All that said, the tools that do exist exist for a reason. They themselves are product solutions that met either an unmet or underserved need. So, ignoring them and going lo-fi for the sake of saying you did is not recommended. You need to look at each individual need, separate from the products that can fix it, and define what you actually want from it.

Let's tackle the tools that I genuinely believe are necessary when building a digital product one by one.

## INTERNAL MESSAGING AND EMAIL

In November of 1996, Mirabilis introduced ICQ (shorthand for "I seek you"). ICQ was a free service that allowed internet users to chat with one another in near real time without having to use e-mail or post to a larger chat room.

In May of 1997, America Online (AOL), at the time the largest online service provider in the United States, launched the initial release of AIM (AOL Instant Messenger). In very short order, pre-teens and teenagers all over the country raced to get usernames they would later regret and drop awkward, vague song lyrics in their "away messages." While there is a lovely nostalgia for me, and I am sure many others, associated with what AIM did in the consumer world, what is often overlooked is the impact it had in the commercial world. The ability to communicate in real time using text via a non-email platform has revolutionized the way business is conducted. Remote working is greatly improved because of it. Transparency between departments and groups can be easily alleviated. Emails can become more focused and less noisy.

For all those reasons, considering how you want to leverage messaging to assist in your product's success should be taken quite seriously. Here is a checklist of questions you should answer while thinking through how messaging does or does not play a role in the success of building your product:

I. Is my team better suited to respond to a number of items all at once or are they better suited to handle issues or questions one by one?

- If all at once, then messaging might be using a tool for the tool's sake. Email, when used appropriately, should be summaries or information and not constant back-and-forth. I will touch on email culture later, but the decisions to be message-centric versus email-centric is one you should make. They both have a place as you work toward building your product, and it might be different team by team, but aligning on what you use messaging for versus what you use email for is an important distinction.

II.   Are there subsets of cross-functional groups within the greater team that will have constant dialogue that is meaningful to easily reference?

-   This question reads as though its slanted toward a "yes." That's because it is. Messaging platforms like Microsoft Teams or Slack have lots of use cases, but this one is one of the most important. The issue with emails is that you get a lot of them and that lots of them are useless. When using a messaging platform, you can preset groups of people to ensure no one is accidentally left off an email thread and try to avoid having to ask your IT team to maintain some twenty email "groups." In doing so, you ensure that pertinent information is in the hands of all the affected parties at the same time and that everyone is given a chance to respond in-line. This can reduce the number of meetings you have, prompt you to have the meetings you actually should have, keep a thorough log of all the information that has been discussed around a particular topic, and ultimately allows you to fairly and justly hold accountable groups and individuals when someone inevitably plays the "I had no idea" card.

III.  What kind of internal SLA (Service Level Agreement) do you want to set for your teams?

-   The thing with having a messaging platform is that it implies quick responses. Messaging is akin to texting, and we all know that one person who can take literal days to respond to something, defeating the purpose of texting in the first place. If immediacy is not something you want your team to be held to, or if it is counter to the culture you want to build, email is the way to go. It will allow your team to take the appropriate time to respond and not leave people on "read," which is a feeling no one enjoys. There is a complication to this if you have a physically dispersed team as opposed to collocated (which I will address in detail later), as not being able to run to someone's desk and get an answer means you will likely need to have some kind of messaging OR you will create an immediacy culture around emails, which is a horrible practice and a good way to get people to quit.

As a guide, if you can answer those three questions, you should be able to decide where in the messaging versus email conversation you fall.

For most everyone it is a combination of both, which is fine. The lesson here is to set expectations around the tools themselves so that everyone is clear on how they should act as well as the standard to which to hold their teammates. The irony of not having good communication around the use of communication tools is thick in many environments, so work ahead of that issue and reap the benefits.

## ROADMAPS

I. Hate. Roadmapping. Tools.

Roadmaps are the bane of many people's existence. They tend to be more hopeful than truthful and often are driven by the need to satisfy clients/investors and not necessarily your users. But they are an extremely important piece of building and managing your product, so you need to buckle in and be ready to create one.

The toolset available for roadmapping usually falls in one of two courts:

**I.**  Development-driven     **II.**  Feature-driven

Development-driven roadmapping tools will tie into your development solutions and try to bucket all the things you have worked on, are working on, and will work on into some kind of Gannt chart.

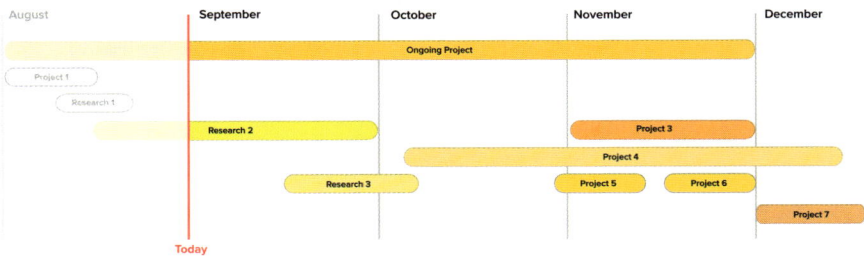

**Gannt Chart**

While that works in theory, it requires a tremendous amount of rigor in your use of the development tools. You will need to have things broken out in very discreet types of development tasks to ensure that you're pulling in only the things that are "roadmap-worthy" and not things that maybe be more tactical in nature or corrections of previously released code. This requires Product Leadership, Project Management, Development and QA all to be highly disciplined around the creation and assignment of tasks.

It also requires you to use a development tracking system that is easily exported into a format you can present or at the very least manipulate for presentation purposes. I will discuss some development task options shortly, but for the purpose of roadmapping, you either have a direct connection that works, or you don't. If it connects in some ways but requires even moderate levels of manual manipulation to get it to a place where it actually serves your need, it is likely that just doing it yourself in the format you require is faster.

While most development tools allow you to create "features," they usually tie back to either releases or groupings of code (often referred to as "Epics" in Kanban speak) that can make pulling them out either laborious or entirely impossible. Because of this, there are large swaths of product roadmapping solutions that exist with the sole intent of creating beautiful roadmaps for you to show people.

Much like development-driven roadmapping, feature-driven roadmapping is usually displayed in some version of a Gannt chart. The major difference here however is that, divorced from the actual work being scheduled and scoped, feature-driven roadmaps tend to be more aspirational. They also tend to be what many start-ups and Entrepreneurs prefer to show, as they are far more seductive than development-driven. But herein lies the issue.

Without the "gut check" of Development, feature-driven roadmaps are always in danger of quickly become vaporware. As a good Product Leader, it should be easy to list out all the things you want your product to do in the future. Memorializing that somewhere is a good thing, if not imperative, so you don't lose sight of it. But putting it on a roadmap implies it is more than desired but is fatally planned.

For that reason, feature-driven roadmapping tools require a great amount of restraint and diligence from Product Leadership. They need to be grounded in reality and constantly checked against the work actually being done. Because of that, you need to be self-effacing and honest. There is a fine line between ambition and deceit.

If you decide to use a feature-driven roadmapping tool, it's important to establish and maintain clear lines as to what the feature is actually intended to impact. The truth of building digital products is that a lot of the work isn't something that materializes for people to see. This is especially true when you are talking to investors/board members/executives. You need to be able to draw a clear line as to what work is being done and what will be done in the future, and you need to be able to speak to the benefit of the work. But oftentimes the benefit of the work may not be something that helps you now. Whether it be refactoring old code, changing to a new code base or platform entirely, or upgrading servers, these tasks are super meaningful and can be a huge benefit to the overall product, but they lack "pizzazz" for that audience. So, it is incumbent on the Product Leader to set the stage in the roadmap for what is driving adoption, usage, or revenue and what is ensuring the stability and sustainability of the platform to allow for the aforementioned items.

Regardless of what tool you do or do not use to create roadmaps, the key is to not lose sight of what a roadmap is actually about, which we'll discuss in greater detail later.

## DEVELOPMENT TRACKING

"You can't manage what you can't measure." These words are rarely met with anything other than a heavy eye roll or exasperated sighs. However, it is an unfortunate truth that the statement is a correct one. And when it comes to building a digital product, measuring is something you will need to do in order to ship.

There are a great many ideologies as to how to break out the work required to actually build a digital product. While those methods were covered earlier, scrum was intentionally left out. For me, scrum belongs here because it's not a process, it is a framework. And that framework can and should have a meaningful effect on how you select your development tracking tool set.

Scrum

"Scrum" is by far the most commonly used methodology. The term first appears in 1986, when management experts Hirotaka Takeuchi and Ikujiro Nonaka published "The New New Product Development Game." The idea of scrum comes from the rugby term, which is when the entire team locks together to propel the ball forward. Hirotaka and Nonaka enjoyed the idea that it took the collaboration of the team to create forward momentum. In 1995, Jeff Sutherland and Ken Schwarber came up with the first scrum process and presented it at the OOPSLA (Object-Oriented Programming, Systems, Languages, and Applications) conference in Texas. In 2001, Sutherland and Schwarber were part of the group that created the earlier mentioned "Manifesto for Agile Software Development."

In 2002, Schwarber founded the Scrum Alliance, where he created a course that outlined what it took to effectively run scrum as a program, and Certified ScrumMasters were born—changing business cards forever.

As mentioned previously, scrum is not actually a process. Scrum is a framework that you can use to guide your development based on the makeup and needs of your individual team. So, as it is the most commonly used framework today, whether practiced with precision or only tangentially, there tends to be enough consistency that we can use some principles as a baseline.

Scrum breaks things down into three discreet elements: Epics, Stories, and Tasks.

An Epic is a large body of work that needs to be broken down into more addressable, actionable undertakings. The entirety of your product could be an Epic itself, or if you are building within a preexisting product and have a larger, new feature or whole new workflow, they would tend to be Epics. Epics usually involve lots of people and a fair amount of description, although not super granular.

A Story is a sub-task within an Epic. The term "Story" is shortened from "user story," which is a term that came from extreme programming in 1998, where instead of "use cases" they actually prescribed the journey of a user through the user's eyes. In doing so, they believed they captured a more practical understanding of what was truly being developed and how it would need to work for it to be considered a success. So, a Story follows a similar ideology here, breaking an Epic down into more approachable, defined articles for your development team to tackle. If the Epic is the entirety of your product, then Stories could be a breakout of individual features. If your Epic is part of a larger product, then the Stories will be a breakout of what makes up that new feature.

Tasks are exactly what they sound like. Tasks are the individual pieces of work that need to be done in order to accomplish a Story. These need to be hyper-prescriptive, so that there is a clear understanding of not only what is being done, but also how it should be done so that it fits into the larger undertaking. Having a culture around "thoughtful and thoroughly written tasks" is something all leaders should strive for. If Tasks are not written well, then the entire construct is meaningless.

Whether you use scrum or not, the above is the modern-day medium for how to best break apart a product into pieces for development. And as most digital shops do leverage scrum, luckily (or unluckily) there is no shortage of development tools supporting it.

So, with that framework in mind, what you need to understand when looking into development tracking tools is what you want the process to be. What that actually means is you can have something as simple and straightforward as this:

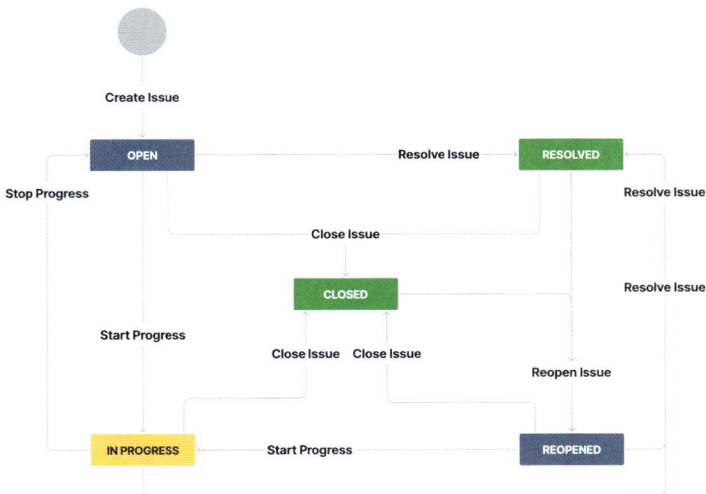

Or something as deliberate and staged as this:

Instead of trying to make your process fit into a solutions framework, here is a list of questions you should answer first:

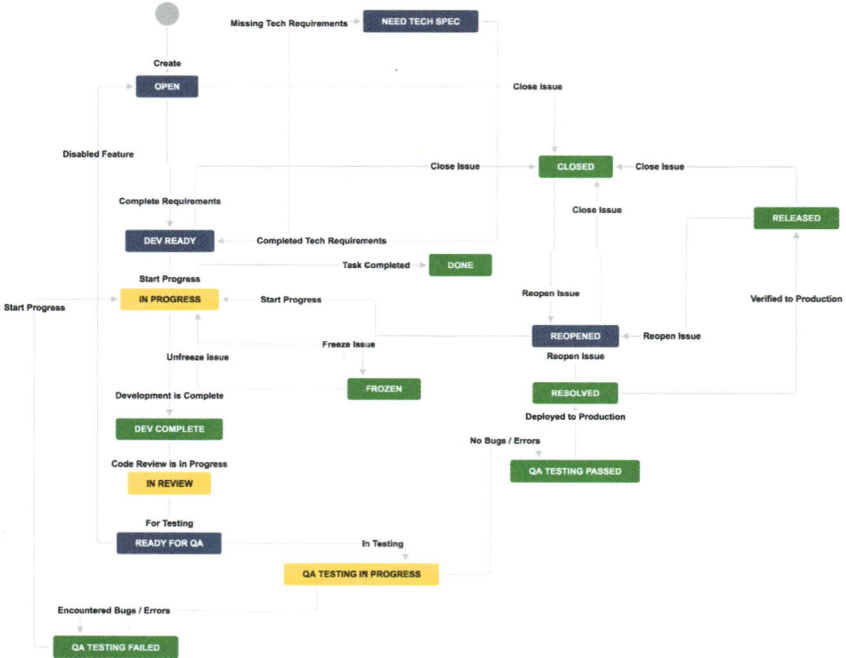

I.   Who in your organization should really be allowed to interact inside of the tool?

-   If you are truly using this tool for development only, then keep as many other disciplines out of the tool as humanly possible. As discussed earlier, giving your Engineers the space to create and not be assaulted with questions and needs is paramount to their success, and allowing too many people into this world can muddy not only their output but also the tool itself.

-   In deciding what roles have access, also decide what their role in the tool will be. Simply saying "you can interact in this" is not enough. Be thoughtful in advance as to what a Product or project person should be able to actually do inside the tool, and more importantly, what they absolutely should not be allowed to do.

- You need to be willing to hurt feelings here. There comes a point in every digital product build where you simply need to hand the keys to your Engineers and let them work. That means no meddling, no input, and only the appropriate amount of visibility to certain team members. While many product and project people bask in the ownership of the things they work on, they need to be kept at the appropriate distance, regardless of all the reasons they tell you they need to know every single detail as the build moves forward.

II. What is the fewest number of steps from ideation to launch your organizational structure can handle?

- This process can be a painful one. So much so that there are a great number of consultancies in the world who will happily charge you upwards of $500 an hour to come in and help define just this one part of the process on your behalf. And if you have a huge organization with lots of legacy job roles and bureaucracy, having someone come in might be the answer. In my experience this can be a pretty simple process if you allow it to be. Here's the exercise:
- List out all the roles that will be allowed within the tool
- Within those roles, write down what each one is responsible for in the journey of building the thing you're building.
  - Here's a super slimmed-down example of what this could look like:

- Product Manager – clearly define the product/feature with enough information to allow development to either scope the level of effort to build or actually begin the process of building. Also responsible for sign-off when feature/product is complete and is ready to be shipped
- Engineer – responsible for the architecture and building of the software based on the requirements delivered. Also responsible for all maintenance, bug fixes, and general stability of the features/products released
- QA – responsible for testing of all code Engineers write prior to being deployed and tested by product. Also responsible for ongoing testing of the product/feature as additional code is released in support of maintenance or new features
- Write a list of all the major responsibilities outlined above, assigning no more than three words to each one
- Write those responsibilities down in chronological order
- Write down the roles that interact in each step, assigning "Owner" to only one role type and "Observer" to any other roles that would need to be aware of the action in this step but are not taking action themselves
- Take yourself out for a nice dinner; you just created your workflow

- This might seem overly simplistic, and the truth is it is. But there is a very distinct reason for that. Trying to create an ideal workflow in advance of knowing how the team is going to work is a fool's errand. What makes the most sense is to clearly know the steps you have to take to get where you're going and to fill in the gaps between them as necessary. Some organizations are served very well with no more than five steps in their development tracking process, whereas some are well served by having upwards of twenty. There is no universal answer. So, own the thought process yourself based on how your team is built and how your company is going to run or runs and let that be what leads the tool, not the other way around.

- It's also very good hygiene to look at this regularly (personally I am a fan of doing this at least quarterly) with the team just to make sure it still makes sense. As teams and products grow, the needs here can change, and making those changes well in advance of them becoming bottlenecks is entirely incumbent on the team knowing enough to take a step back and look.

III. What level of investment are you truly willing to put forth to define and execute against the choice you make?

- This is a hard one because it is by nature a premature ask. You have no idea how seriously you are going to take this practice prior to actually implementing it. Your heart and head might be in a place where you are certain this is going to be religion in your organization, but the practical application of a tool and the actual effectiveness of a tool are two very,

very different things. So, this exercise is a meaningful one, because this is not just about capital investment, it's about time and energy as well.

- Capital Investment

    - The majority of the development tracking tools in the world will offer super affordable solutions for smaller organizations. But, as with all things, paying less means getting less. And most often the "less" you get from these tools isn't the tearing out of functionality or of features but instead the limiting of the ability of the users to customize the toolset. This is a huge deal. As we have just discussed, your organization is going to be different from others. There is no "one-size-fits-all" in this space. And so if you go through the exercise above or something like it and land on a process you truly believe will best suit your organization, even if that process is a streamlined one, you might find yourself in a position where you are asked to pay more do to less. While this likely will (and reasonably so) make you clench your fists and grind your teeth, it very well might be what needs to happen. If you have been thoughtful and thorough in your assessment of the process you desire and you find yourself unable to fund a tool that allows for it out of the box, paying extra to get it just how you wish is something I'd strongly consider. "Close enough" when it comes to processes like this is very rarely close enough, so weigh the actual upfront capital for just getting it done out of the gate against what will happen if you find out you weren't "close enough" and need to start all over.

- This tool in particular is not one that gets changed out often, if ever, in most organizations. You are going to put a tremendous amount of data through it, and that data can help shape your organization tremendously. There are other toolsets which can be done on the cheap or can be changed out without serious implications to the organization (roadmapping tools, for instance). So do proper due diligence on features, analytics, support, and SLA's when looking into development tracking with an understanding that this is software you are marrying, not dating. And divorces can be ugly.

- Human Capital Investment

  - These tools take time. They take time to implement, they take time to maintain, they take time to successfully train people on. These are soft costs which cannot be ignored when it comes to your decision around tool selection. The extent to which you can pass some or all of these responsibilities off on the company that provides the tool to you is great (although will cost you actual capital), but I have never worked somewhere where there wasn't someone in-house who was the defacto development tool expert. Thinking about this in advance can not only help you select the right tool but also help you identify the internal resources that will ultimately be responsible for ensuring the success of the tool itself.

- Implementation
    - Make sure you have clear responsibility laid out for who owns implementation and maintenance of the actual technology itself. Chances are no one will volunteer, but it needs to be "owned."
- Training
    - Create a very clear training program in advance. Again, be sure that you assign clear ownership. Whether it be something provided to you by your vendor or something you need to create in-house, make sure there is human-readable documentation that can be easily accessed by anyone in your organization who is expected to engage with the tool. I also highly recommend recording a video walkthrough right out of the gate so that there is a reference for people to check back in on. As all the tools in this space tend to have plenty to navigate between, screenshots will make documentation enormous and potentially hard to navigate. Creating video content where users can explicitly see what they need to do for a given task is not only super-serving your

users but will save you countless hours of troubleshooting.

IV.  What do we expect to learn from this tool?

- A very often overlooked piece when looking into these tools is what you can do with the data the tool generates. Thinking about how much information is being pushed into a development tracking tool is only part of the conversation you should be having. You should also proactively be thinking about what kind of data is being created by the tool. There is invaluable information that can be gleaned from these systems. Things as high-level as measuring time between creation and completion of tasks or as granular as tracking individual role and function dwell time on particular types of tasks. These data points can assist in your resource planning, your hiring practice, or even go as far as to change the way your teams hand tasks and projects off between groups. While the goal should never be to use these tools as a spying mechanism, ignoring the data that they provide would be negligent. So, take time in advance to think through how to ensure the tool is configured to be able to properly generate these data points.

Development tracking is arguably the most important tool you will purchase when building a digital product. When implemented correctly, it is the engine that that creates power from the fuel that is your product. If implemented incorrectly or not at all, it can be the reason your Engineering team is unable to successful complete their task.

In many cases, less truly is more, but less means less, not nothing. Whether this be a tool you create or a tool you purchase is irrelevant, but having a process in place and a tool to track that process is non-negotiable. Take the selection of this seriously, and you will expedite your path to successfully launching digital products.

## BEYOND MISSION STATEMENTS: THE POWER OF PRACTICAL MANTRAS

"Never half-ass two things, whole-ass one thing" is a wonderful quote from Ron Swanson on *Parks and Recreation*. It's a delightful reminder that remaining focused on the endgame is a key component to effectively building a product. In the digital ecosystem, as complex as it is and as frequently as it changes, it is very easy to find yourself somewhere that is not on the path you want to be on. There is a tremendous amount of "noise" that can infiltrate your thinking when building a digital solution, much of which has already been discussed. So, while a quote from Ron Swanson might sound more like a joke than it does something to be taken seriously, I assure you the lesson is a critical one.

As companies are founded today, a standard practice is to come up with a Mission Statement. A Mission Statement is defined as a formal summary of the aims and values of a company, organization, or individual. There are entire consultancies that are focused exclusively on being able to help craft Mission Statements. It's meant to reflect the pillars of a company or a product, the north star, if you will. Something to always look to in order to ensure the thing you are working on is getting you closer to fulfilling your mission.

While I take no direct issue with Mission Statements, they tend to get very marketing focused. Guy Kawasaki, the former Chief Evangelist of Apple and present Chief Evangelist of Canva, said in a TEDx talk at Berkeley in 2014 that companies should focus on "Mantras," not Mission Statements. His example was Wendy's, whose Mission Statement at the time was "to deliver superior quality products and services for our customers and communities through leadership, innovation, and partnerships." This perfectly exemplifies the issue I have with Mission Statements. As Guy points out, never once going through a Wendy's do you think to yourself, "Man, I feel like I have gained a better understanding of leadership, innovation, and partnership." What you got was fed. So, Guy suggests Wendy's should instead have a Mantra of "healthy fast food"—something simple, tangible, and actionable that fits exactly what it is you are trying to do.

What does that have to do with you "whole-assing" one thing? Everything. The idea of a product Mantra is an important one, especially in the digital world. Being able to succinctly tell someone what it is your product does in five or fewer non-confusing words will not only help you immensely as you test and release your product, but should be a constant thought as you are building. And as such, at every feature you come across, you should ask yourself, "Does someone already do this one thing really well that would allow me to do what I want either more affordably, faster, or better?" If you are honest with yourself, unless you are on the edge of true invention, the answer is likely yes for a lot of what you are building. But the collection of parts and how they come together is most often the magic in digital.

In larger organizations, this exercise is often referred to as "Build, buy, or partner." It's an exercise where you weigh the financial and timeline impact of building out a feature as opposed to partnering or buying the technology elsewhere. It should be a process that the Product Owner facilitates wherein you offer a thoroughly detailed analysis of the pros and cons of each scenario and offer your opinion as to which is most likely to positively impact the product for your users.

For the vast majority of products, "buy" is off the table, which leaves you with only "build" and "partner." The inclination of most of the Engineers I have worked with will always be to build, especially when it needs to be a part of the larger solution they are crafting. This is where we get to "whole-assing one thing." If resources and timelines were no object, it should be the opinion of every Product Owner that you should build it exactly as your product requires. To put it mildly, that is rarely—if ever—the case. It is more likely you have aggressive timelines and very finite resources, so instead you need to make decisions as to what makes your product YOUR product and be, at the very least, willing to explore anything that is already being done well by someone else.

Let's use authenticated sign-on as a straightforward example, as we have already touched on it earlier when discussing partnerships. If you are building an online application meant for the masses, building out the infrastructure of sign-on, what to the end user looks like a menial task is not a small lift. It requires you to build rules and logic around usernames and passwords, securely store the information, create workflows for retrieving the information if forgotten, provide support when your workflow fails, etc. All of this is a strain on your resources, which could otherwise be used to tackle tasks more specific to your product.

Another reason I chose this example is to remind you to never lose sight of your user. Think about the number of usernames and passwords you have in your life. Do you dread every time you log in to something from a new device where you don't have that information saved? How many times a year would you say you have to reset a password? If you are anything like me, it's a lot. So, looking at something like sign-on from the user standpoint, if there is a way to allow them to use something that they are more likely to remember or have saved, why would you not do that? Even if it would be roughly the same amount of work to integrate as it would be to build it out, making the user's life easier should always win, which means you and your team casting your egos aside and doing what's right.

Being inflexible in how you deliver to your endgame is a recipe for headaches and letdowns. Take the creation of your Mantra seriously and put it on the walls of your office, on the background of your desktop, in every meeting room you have, and if at any point you find yourself splitting your time between a single feature or function and the overall product, it's time to take a long hard look at whatever that is and figure out how to better solution it.

The reason you use these tools is to avoid the one big thing that disrupts Product Owners more than anything else: **surprises**.

# High Tolerance for the Truth and No Surprises

## 12

T he reason you use these tools is to avoid the one big thing that disrupts Product Owners more than anything else: surprises. The hard truth is that there is absolutely nothing you can do to prevent being surprised in development. Absolutely nothing. It is at the core of building a digital product. Things you did not anticipate are going to happen and things you simply could not anticipate are going to happen. So be aware of that as truth, accept it, and prepare for how to handle it.

How you handle it is everything. And this is not a product feature, but a tenet of your product culture. The term "high tolerance for the truth and no surprises" has been with me for almost my entire professional career. The second part of that sentence might feel like it is in direct opposition to how I started this chapter. As a stand-alone statement, it would be. But paired with the first part, it is why I believe this to be one of the most important constants in building a successful product culture and organization.

"High tolerance for the truth." It reads as innocent and straightforward, needing little to no additional explanation. I assure you, that is not the case. Putting those words into practice is hard. Actually, real life hard. And it's something you absolutely have to do if you are going to survive building digital products. Here's why.

## USERS/CLIENTS

One of the many tricky things about delivering user-centric software is the users themselves. The truth is most people have no idea how to solve the problem at hand, but they know they want it solved . . .until you solve it. Then you will get all kinds of input as to how you should have solved it better.

We talked about how to get users involved via testing and focus groups, and that is extremely important. Equally important is that when you do exactly what they ask you to do, make all the changes precisely as they requested, and hear that word that sends shivers down the spine of anyone who asks for feedback on something they built—"Actually . . ."— you are open to it, okay with it, and at peace with re-working your re-work for the greater good.

If you have ever cooked for children, you are ready for this moment.

You: "What do you want to eat?"

Child: "Literally anything in the world."

You, after making the thing they want: "Here you go."

Child: "I don't like this thing I explicitly asked for, I actually want this."

In that moment, you have three very distinct options.

I.    You can argue that you did exactly as asked, reminding the child that they in fact wanted this very thing not more than ten minutes ago, hoping to spark their memory. The outcome of this is either the child eating something they don't actually mind but decided they didn't want in lieu of something else, or the child not eating it because it actually wasn't something they liked at all, and how dare you for not knowing better than them what they do and do not like.

II. You can acknowledge that they don't like the thing they asked for anymore, or never did, and tell them it is the only way they get any food at all. This is you openly and honestly communicating to them that in this moment their need for what they actually want is not going to cut it and they need to make do with what exists, or they can die hungry.

III. You eat the thing you made for them, make them the new thing they asked for, making it clear that there was no "next thing," accepting that there was wasted time in this for you and wasted energy on both sides, but ultimately getting the kid what they wanted and not being all that worse off for it, even if the first thing would have done just fine.

In building products, the desire to do number I will exist fervently and often. You will constantly want to push back when people take shots at things you have changed and decisions you have made after incorporating the feedback they themselves gave. But you need to resist that urge and instead lean into a response more like number II or III.

Response II, while it might read as apathetic, can actually be delivered with empathy. It is based in honesty, when something simply cannot be changed or done in a given situation. If delivered in such a manner and delivered by a person or a company with a track record of being honest and forthcoming, the blow can be significantly lessened, to the point of it being appreciated.

Response III is on the table much less often. In the rarest of cases can you just throw away work and changes and do something different on a whim without upsetting the flow of development, the expectation of investment or leadership, and without negatively impacting timelines. When the opportunity does present itself, I highly encourage you embrace and bask in it, because there are few things in building products that will fulfill you more than getting to say "We absolutely can" to your users for something they want.

The key takeaway here is that in both responses II and III you are leading with the truth. It is not argumentative, manipulative, condescending, or adversarial. It is just what is happening, delivered in such a way that is clear, concise, and honest. Communicating with your users from the beginning that you will message with that level of honesty, that level of candor, and that you will do so early and often sets the stage for the remainder of your relationship.

You are going to experience outages and issues. If you make a point to quickly and honestly let your users know instead of frantically ignoring tweets or direct messages hoping you will have it fixed, even if you lose people over the issue, you did not mislead them. That kind of truth, over time, creates loyalty and trust that affords you luxuries you cannot begin to measure.

## PARTNERS

As we have previously discussed, building in the digital world most often involves some kind of partnership. And, just like with your users, how you communicate with partners will shape your company and your product. The digital world is all so tied together, both in the literal and figurative sense, that creating sound partnerships goes far beyond simply affording your users functionality or data they want. It can literally be something that defines your company.

There is a high probability that if you are partnering with another company, you are not the only one. Very often you will interact with Partner Channel Managers (or some similar title), whose sole role it is to work with other companies, assess if the partnership is a favorable one for the optics and finances of their company, build and negotiate contracts, and eventually help with the onboarding process of the partner. These folks are gatekeepers to functionality/data that you have expressed you need for your product, so establishing a relationship based on trust and transparency is paramount. The obvious reason is that it rarely pays off to be an asshat, but the reasons are actually much deeper than that.

## SERVICE LEVEL

Along with the Partner Channel Manager will generally come some version of a Technical Account Manager (TAM). While the Partner Channel Manager will handle the business side of things, eventually you will need to dive into the technicality of the partnership. At that point, you will be handed off directly to the TAM or someone on the team who can handle the technical components of a conversation.

This person will be your shepherd in making the integration actually work. This person is important to you. Very important.

In all my years of doing this, I can count on one hand how many times I have encountered documentation so tight and specific that it required absolutely no follow-up whatsoever. It is standard fare to need to check in with someone who is an expert on the thing you are integrating with from time to time.

Enter the "high tolerance for the truth and no surprises" construct. Just like the Partner Channel Manager is likely dealing with more than one client, the TAM is the same. And having a TAM who appreciates how you work and is on the road with you to help can save you almost immeasurable amounts of time. Be it pushing you up in the queue or just being super responsive to you the second you ask a question, being in the good graces of these folks is well worth the time. So, setting that stage early can be the difference. Here are some steps to take in the early stages of the relationship to ensure you get their buy-in and appreciation.

I.  Tell them how you work

  ▪ Giving insight into how your organization actually works can be super helpful. If you operate in Sprints or are a Continuous Development shop, tell them. You don't need to open the kimono and show them your development tracking boards, but having insight into your cadence can help to set their expectations as to when you will likely pop up in their world.

II.   Have questions ready on the first call

- Just like you, these folks are busy. And the first call is a litmus test as to how easy or what a pain in the ass you are likely going to be. So, prior to ever getting on the call with the TAM, push the Partner Channel Manager to give you as much documentation as you can, and genuinely spend some time with it. Don't just peruse it, read through it. Note where there are things you don't understand. Note the things that you don't think pertain to you and have them clearly outlined so you can confirm that your assumptions are correct. We live in a world where documentation can sometimes turn into a "look how much we wrote" show, and often much of it might be meaningless to your cause, so spend the time making sure that is not the case.

III.   When you're entering development, set up regular touch bases

- I cannot stress enough how huge this can be, and how much easier it can make it for both sides. Put fifteen minutes on the books every week to just quickly touch base. Make sure to send your questions over at least one day prior to the call. Why send the questions in advance of the call? If they can be answered over email and you can skip the call, awesome—you are a hero and gave them time back. If the questions can't be, you have time already set aside to talk through it, as opposed to having to get time on the books. It also signals to your partner you intend on doing this right and paying attention. The key here is to not schedule these until you are ready.

# REPUTATION

One thing that never ceases to amaze me is that no matter what industry I have worked in or around, they have always been small. Not in the sense of the dollars they generate, or the volume of code and technology they produce, but the communities that surround them. As the information age and the digital world has taught us, the world is smaller than you think. And business is absolutely no exception.

Being known as being easy to work with is a weapon in your arsenal that you simply cannot put a value on. Whether it be getting people to engage with you at all, asking for referrals, or even helping you move into new roles or organizations, your reputation is huge. And working well with partners is an enormous part of that.

Remind yourself where your partner sits in the ecosystem. They are likely working with all kinds of other companies and people to offer a solution similar to or the same as the one you need. Inherently, that means they have large networks of people within your space— your competitors, companion applications or websites, and likely the capital world.

Because of this, being transparent and forthcoming with them can have enormous downstream effects for your company, your product, and you personally. They are perfectly positioned to be town criers. So, you need to be mindful of setting them, and your team, up for success from the beginning. Here's how.

I.   Make a timeline and change it as needed

   ▪   Giving your partner a timetable for when you will be working on the parts that affect them is a must. It will rarely be the only thing you have in development, which means it will be battling against other features or issues for attention. That means that it is likely to be fluid—specifically if you are building other functionality around it. That means there is opportunity for dates to change and slip—and that's okay. But it's only okay if you tell your partner that when you deliver the first timeline and then subsequently update that throughout the process. That doesn't mean you tell them once the dates have slipped. That means you tell them the instant you think the dates might slip. High tolerance for the truth and no surprises. Remember they are also running a business, with finite resources and multiple clients. They have testing and resources on their side that they will set up to ensure things are working as intended for you. If you alert them to dates changing, they can adjust and do their best to not disrupt their business. If you are not ready the day of testing, you put them in a tough position, and greatly decrease their desire to help you and your company out in the future.

II.  Pad your dates

   ▪   Along with giving dates to your partners in advance, give yourself and your team a bit more time than you think you'll need. This will benefit you for a number of reasons. It will help you not be in the position mentioned above, which is the biggest one. The ancillary benefit is you might be ready early. This is a win because you can tell your partner that, which will look great. I have also found that very often if you are ready to go early, you partner will love to accommodate that, because they have other clients who are slipping dates that they could push back into your spot. This flows beautifully into your reputation as on top of your game and being accommodating.

III.   Be gracious, be grateful

- The partner world is often one of high volume and quick churn. Things like messaging or data services, which are usually tied into a much larger vision of a product, can sometimes feel like something you want to breeze through and give little thought to. But be mindful that when you are on the phone or in a meeting with your partner, it is the thing that they do. Sometimes it's the one and only thing. So, don't dismiss this as something trivial or just a piece of something bigger. Be grateful that someone else has made this thing so well that it wasn't worth your time to make it yourself. Be grateful that they are passionate and making the time to ensure that you use it the right way. Be gracious with your admiration and acknowledgment of them taking the time.

## EMPLOYEES/TEAMS

Building digital products is a team sport. You cannot do it alone. Not if it's going to be a meaningful product. It requires teams. And as we covered earlier, depending on the roles and personality types, those teams need and expect different things from you as a Product Leader. But if there is one thing they all have in common, it is that they will all benefit from you running the organization with a "high tolerance for the truth and no surprises" mindset. This simple and somewhat pithy saying can absolutely change the way your company or team functions. If truly embraced, it allows for a forum of free speech and collaboration that can define an organization, and I have found in my career that those kinds of cultures translate to the best products.

"High tolerance for the truth and no surprises," when it comes to your team, means walking away from a culture of fear and punishment. It means fostering and believing in a culture that not only welcomes someone raising their hand and saying, "I fucked up, and this is going to be the effect," but lifting them up as a pillar of heroism when they do. It means empowering every single person on your team to be in control of their own lane and having the support from you and the team around them to fail.

This does not translate to an absence of accountability. There are consequences for every action, and you should run your teams the same way. But if you can truly lean into this construct, not just in principle but in practice, the volume of mistakes and gravity of them is likely to be much smaller.

What I have observed when this practice is in place is that communication increases exponentially. When people are empowered to own things, that ownership means something to them. It resonates with them on a personal level. And with an entire team in a similar headspace, you create a space where it is safe for people to ask for help early and often. The idea that you own something doesn't mean you are doing it alone; it means you are responsible for its success. But that responsibility is not only on your shoulders, and creating an environment that encourages people to raise their hand and go "I made a mistake" is the same environment that will lead people to raise their hand in advance and go "I think I'm about to screw this up" or "I'm stuck on how to get this one thing done."

In an environment like the one I'm describing, the accountability comes when you don't raise your hand early enough. It comes when you stay within and don't remain aware of where you have actually gotten yourself. It comes with being so far down the rabbit hole the team needs an excavator to dig you out. It comes from being careless and not thinking through something that the rest of the team had entrusted to you.

It never comes from asking too many questions. It never comes from being stuck. It never comes from being frustrated and feeling like you don't know how to dig yourself out. All of those things, when addressed early and honestly, are almost encouraged. Time and time again I have seen in those moments, regardless of the discipline, groups of people working together and laughing and ribbing one another, but in the end solutioning.

This philosophy creates an entire culture around teachable moments. When someone is stuck somewhere and feels comfortable saying so immediately instead of wasting a week or more on trying to figure it out, they go to their peers and ask for help. If this is truly done right, that peer (not always a superior, by the way, but often it can be) will ask the entire group if they also would struggle with this issue. If that answer is yes, you get the group together and discuss it as a team, so on the other side of this issue, not only has one person learned, but the entire team has. And by fostering moments like this, you could find brand new solutions to issues by inviting people into the conversation.

When I say that building digital products is a team sport, it truly is. In this context, it most resembles football. As the CEO/Product Owner, you are the quarterback. It is your job to select the play, clearly communicate it to your teammates, and execute. Each of the players on the field have their own responsibility, and success occurs when each individual can thrive in their task. If you have an offensive lineman who is getting absolutely hammered by a linebacker but doesn't feel safe enough to bring that up in the huddle, you, the QB, get hit. It might not be the linebacker who gets you; it could be a defensive lineman who gets free because someone else slides in to help his teammate. But the difference here is if that decision is made in the moment, you are exposed. If that decision is made ahead of time, you can adjust accordingly. And that entire team takes their signal from the QB. If you get back in the huddle after blowing your assignment and hear "Do your job!" from the QB, chances that you ask for help are slim to none. If you get back in the huddle and hear "High tolerance for the truth—do you need help out there?", you might just hear what someone actually needs to succeed.

The way you do anything is the way you do everything. It is succinct and simple. It immediately shows you its intent.

It is non-negotiable.

# The Way You Do Anything Is the Way You Do Everything

**13**

This is likely not the first time you are hearing this quote. It has been accredited to Zen Buddhists and many other religions, meditative practices, and countless upon countless people. I first heard it from a CEO years ago. And while my intention has been to avoid topics that have been exhaustedly covered, this one I believe deserves airtime, but in a more precise way than I have observed elsewhere.

There is profound beauty in this quote even at the highest level. It is succinct and simple. It immediately shows you its intent. It is non-negotiable. Whether you subscribe to it or not, it is perfectly contained within itself. It is the perfect product, in language form.

Similar to the previous chapter, putting this into practice is entirely different from subscribing to it shallowly. In order to really dive into this, we first need to understand the concept of "signaling." This is about to get a bit odd, but come with me on this.

In biology, there are four different types of chemical "signaling" among cells. Autocrine, where a cell targets itself, paracrine, where a cell targets a nearby cell, signaling across gaps, where a cell targets another cell connected by gap junctions, and endocrine, where a cell targets a distant cell through the bloodstream. We are going to focus on paracrine and endocrine signaling.

Paracrine signals between cells move by diffusion through the extracellular matrix. These signals are quick bursts of information from one cell to another that are gone as quickly as they arrive. An example of a paracrine signal is the transfer of signals across synapses between nerve cells—so, moving. Because of the short distance between them, information can very quickly be sent across cells and elicit an almost immediate response. Once that response has been received, enzymes and neighboring cells will help to degrade those signals, in essence removing them from existence in short order. In other words, a clear and concise message was sent, acted on by the intended party, and then appropriately ignored by others.

Endocrine signals are very different. As opposed to sending signals from cell to cell, endocrine signals are sent over large distances through the bloodstream to other target cells. This process is much slower than that of the paracrine path, and because of this transport method, some of the signal is lost through travel. Just as they take longer to reach their destination, endocrine signals also have a longer-lasting impact. Endocrine cells affect the thyroid, hypothalamus, and pituitary glands, making them responsible for the creation of hormones. Hormones are produced in the aforementioned cells but affect other body regions far away from the actual glands themselves. In other words, decisions are made elsewhere in the system and eventually find their way to the intended recipient. Because those signals traveled far, the message can be less clear, leaving ambiguity on the receiver's end.

What does this have to do with digital products? I will explain.

## DECODING PARACRINE SIGNALS: UNDERSTANDING SUBTLE COMMUNICATION

To bring another famous quote into the equation, "It's the little things." When I think about "The way you do anything is the way you do everything," my immediate thought is about all the small, seemingly fleeting moments that go by throughout a day. Did I smile at that person as they walked past me this morning? I should have held that door for the person behind me. Did I ask anyone else if they wanted anything from the cafe when I went out today?

All those small, intimate gestures that can change the path of someone's day entirely—those are the first to come to mind when I observe this quote. And those little things, over the course of the day, amount to big things. So, it is a worthwhile exercise to examine how you can best set up your team to be aware of those little moments.

## IT STARTS WITH YOU

You set the tone for your team or your organization. From the moment you walk in the door, all those small things are being observed by everyone around you. So, it is your job—actually part of your job—to be aware of it. Say good morning to people, even when you are having a bad day. Shit, tell them you're having one of those mornings where you just aren't into it. It won't stay with them long, but that kind of honesty and openness in a passing greeting is a signal that you are honest and open. Be the person who asks if anyone needs anything from the cafe. Be the person who recommends a great book about dog training you used because you heard someone just got a puppy. Make a point to put birthdays in YOUR calendar so you remember to celebrate the people on your team. And consider reaching out to them alone, not making it a public thing. You want them to know YOU wanted to say it, not that you want everyone else to see you do it. It means more one on one, always.

## CREATE SMALL MOMENTS

Office birthday parties are the stuff of legend. The same cake, weird hats, a half-hearted rendition of "Happy Birthday." Same goes for hitting the gong when a big sale goes through. All these things are good, and I'm not suggesting you stop them, but they are expected. As the leader, you have the ability to bring joy and laughter whenever you want. Be silly. Make dance videos and send them out to your team. Wear absurd costumes for no particular reason. Make up fake holidays and get people to participate. There are no rules against having a good time. And when you do these things—these small, fleeting things that break up the day and make people think, "they're nuts" or "what a weirdo"—you are sending this fast burst of signals that that kind of energy is allowed. You are reminding everyone that it's okay to hold doors, or dance, or laugh, or cry. If this isn't who you are, that's okay. Find someone who it is and encourage them to do it. The point is to show your team that there is room for kindness and silliness in their work. This is not a distraction. These are reminders that everyone is human and lives a life outside of what you do for work.

## PRACTICE "THANK YOU"

"Thank you." Two of the most powerful words in the English language. When delivered earnestly, they can actually change your physical chemistry. As part of your company or team's essence, encourage and acknowledge the practice of saying thank you. This seems trivial, I know, but it's not. Creating discipline around being thankful and showing that thanks to your colleagues is the opposite of trivial. If you know that someone stepped in to help someone who was struggling with a task, thank them personally. If someone went above and beyond and saved the day, thank them publicly. These are moments that quickly fade, like the ones mentioned above, but the signals here are so meaningful. When you thank someone, you are doing more than just being grateful for something they did for you. You are signaling that you are aware of the effort. You are signaling to them that you were paying attention at a level they might not have assumed. You are signaling to everyone else that they should pay attention on that level as well. These are not long-lasting, but over time, with enough of them, patterns will emerge to your team.

## THE ENDOCRINE EFFECT: INFLUENCING SILENTLY

As mentioned, endocrine signals take longer to be received but have longer-term effects. In relation to business, these signals might not feel like signals at all. They might just feel like standard business practices that need to occur in order for your team to get the job done. But believe me, they are signals. They are signals as to how your team feels you and the organization feel about them as people. These signals, much like puberty, are confusing and not always easy to understand, especially if you have great practice around paracrine signaling. I want to highlight the three largest endocrine-style signals I most commonly see being sent and how to address them.

## MEETING CULTURE

Have you ever sat in a meeting and about five minutes in thought to yourself, "This probably could have been an email"? Have you ever sat through six of them in the same day? When you let your organization or team develop a culture of having meetings around everything, you are signaling to all of them that they cannot be trusted to make decisions and get the work done without supervision. In the beginning, it might not feel that way. When starting work, it makes sense to be in a room together to have conversations and setting direction. But if those meetings persist, if you have teams that are constantly in rooms together discussing how and what to work on, the signal is that they can't do it without guidance. And over time, that signal will become more and more evident to them, and it will create hostility and mistrust.

This also pulls people away from doing the work they signed up for, and that they (hopefully) take pride in. When you remove the option for people to be productive in their actual roles but still hold them accountable to timetables and standards, they are handcuffed. Again, signaling that they can't produce without oversight.

There is a time and place for meetings. They are unavoidable. And they should not be avoided. With the proper execution of meetings, people should look forward to them, because when they are invited to one it should be something they have a vested interest in. But abusing meetings as a way to manage people, or check in, or—worst of all—appear to be "busy," is a clear signal that you don't value your team's ability or time.

It is incumbent entirely on you as a leader to monitor the company's meeting practices. If certain business units or individuals are creating large meetings with large groups regularly, check in with the attendees and make sure they feel the meetings are productive. Talk directly to the person scheduling the meetings and ask them what the intention of the meeting is, and if they feel there are other ways to achieve it.

The single biggest commodity your team trades in is time, so make it your job to not only actively ensure that they have as much time as possible, but that they observe you monitoring the process and policy of your organization as well, so that the signal is omnipresent.

## VACATION/LEAVE POLICIES

While most companies in the US have a pretty simple calculation of this, the digital world has had an absolute field day creating new and creative ways to get people really excited about vacation policies. It is lauded as a huge perk for young potential candidates that you can receive "unlimited vacation" when joining many of the upstart digital companies. But before we dive into what that actually looks like, let's look at the history.

In 1910, President William Howard Taft proposed that all American workers should be given two to three months off "in order to continue his work next year with that energy and effectiveness which it ought to have." He was quoted in the New York Times as saying, "The American people have found out that there is such a thing as exhausting the capital of one's health and constitution." Perhaps not surprisingly, most large organizations took exception to President Taft's comments, citing that there was no way they could produce at the necessary levels with those kinds of resources being stripped away.

While there was no legislation enacted from President Taft's bold assertion, the early twentieth century did show a large number of employers offering time off for workers. In the 1920s, high-end department stores would arrange for their employees to have paid vacations at seashore camps. In the 1930s and 1940s, with the rise of unions, vacation coverage for hourly employees had gown to almost 50 percent. During World War II, companies began to use vacation time as a way to bolster the total compensation package to attract talent while maintaining lower salaries to offset the Depression.

That attitude to offering vacation but taking away additional benefits would quietly shape the vacation and leave landscape in the US for years to come. While many other nations have long supported seven- to eight-week standard vacation policies (Germany and Sweden, for instance) the US has long since adopted and maintained the "standard two weeks and one of sick leave."

**The US is still light-years behind in maternity leave**
Total weeks of paid leave available to mothers (full-rate equivalent)*

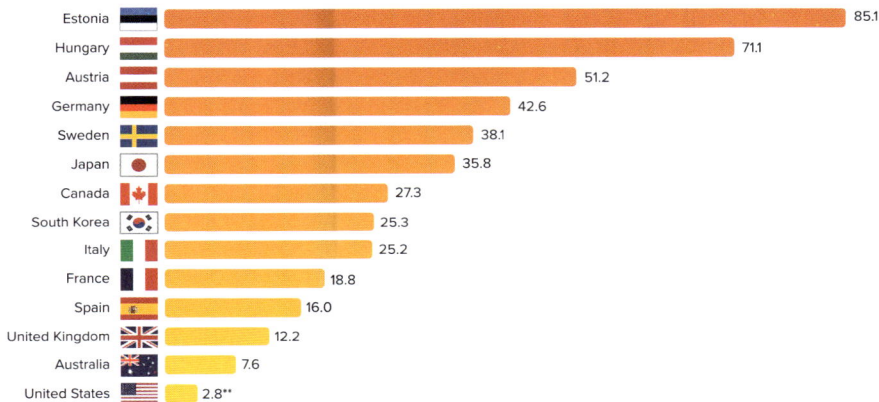

| Country | Weeks |
|---|---|
| Estonia | 85.1 |
| Hungary | 71.1 |
| Austria | 51.2 |
| Germany | 42.6 |
| Sweden | 38.1 |
| Japan | 35.8 |
| Canada | 27.3 |
| South Korea | 25.3 |
| Italy | 25.2 |
| France | 18.8 |
| Spain | 16.0 |
| United Kingdom | 12.2 |
| Australia | 7.6 |
| United States | 2.8** |

*Weeks are presented as full-rate equivalent (total length of leave entitlement multiplied by the average wage replacement rate.
**Trump has proposed 6 weeks paid leave - an average of 2.8 weeks of benefits in terms of a full-rate wage equivalent

*Source: Statista*

But it's not just vacation, it's leave in general. The most controversial and covered of this is not about your leisure time but instead the length of maternity and the mere existence of paternity leave. The US is known worldwide for not only allowing for less, but also for not mandating any, time off when a mother gives birth. This is then extended when you look at the number of US companies that offer adoptive mothers reasonable maternity time or meaningful paternity packages.

The point of all of this is not to bash the lack of federal US policy but instead to shine a light on the fact that it is very much in your control as a leader to not only create but enforce thoughtful and reasonable vacation and leave policies.

In 2019 over 768 million vacation days went unused in the US according to the "Time Off and Vacation Usage" report released by the US Travel Association. Of those 768 million, they estimate that over 236 million would be lost completely and not be able to be carried over. That's over $65.5 billion in lost benefits. While that might appeal to your CFO and investors, it does not bode well for building a company and product culture that is not only sustainable and scalable but also attracts top tier talent.

Just like meeting culture, vacation and leave culture starts at the top. In a survey of 1,200 American workers, Kimble Applications found that there are four main reasons people don't use their available vacation time:

I.    Vacations cause more stress – 27 percent of respondents feel like they simply can't walk away without coming back to a nightmare scenario. In my experience, this is largely due to lack of communication around time off in advance and proper team planning.

II.   Thanks to technology, it's harder than ever to unplug – we covered some of this already and will cover more in the next section, but the fact that you can reach your employees at your whim does not mean you should. And in many cases, doing so will have the opposite effect than you intend.

III.  "It'll derail my career" – 14 percent believe that not taking vacations will lead to them being seen as more interested, more invested, and therefore more worthy of being acknowledged and promoted. This is entirely cultural.

IV.   "My boss doesn't like it" – 19 percent of respondents leave time they "earn" on the table because they believe their boss doesn't actually want them to take the time.

While all of the above are directly related to how you set up your company and product culture, that last one makes me genuinely angry. It is very easy to tell your colleagues and employees you care about them. It is easy to install "unlimited vacation" policies. But the only thing that truly matters is that you stand behind the language you write on the page. In the absence of that, I would argue you would be better off simply stating that you get two weeks vacation and one week of sick time, but truly sticking to it.

Like the other endocrine signals, this starts at the top. If you have a motor that does not require time off, that is okay, and you should not be punished for it. Specifically, if you are a founder or executive team member, your earning potential might make the value exchange of your time worthwhile. But that will not be true for everyone. And even for folks who have as much or more to gain, needing to step away to gain clarity and perspective is not a weakness.

This then also extends to maternity/paternity/bereavement. This topic is polarizing for a number of reasons, and instead of diving deeply into my personal opinions on the matter, I want to simply address how you position whatever your position is. There is a common practice in referring to work teams as "families," and sometimes that might very well be the case. However, the truth is that everyone on your team also has some version of a family outside your organization. Both legally and out of common decency and respect, your view into that life is entirely up to them, and it should be. But when deciding on the level of leave to give to expecting parents or grieving colleagues, do your best to imagine yourself in those shoes, even if you have never been there.

So, when putting together your vacation and leave packages, think about the long-term signaling you are doing. If you know that, based on the growth and acceleration of your company, an unlimited vacation policy is unreasonable, don't enact one. Instead, promise people what you are truly comfortable guaranteeing and enact a process for requesting additional time as needed. If you truly expect and require everyone to work at the level you are willing to in order to launch your company or product, then stipulate that early as well, and compensate people either monetarily or with time when you have achieved your goal.

The other signal that's important to send is how you treat your time. As I previously mentioned, if you have never-ending gas for your product, that is perfectly okay, but maybe sometimes do it from home. In the digital age, there is literally no reason to schlep into an office if you are sick. The idea that you are showing "commitment and strength" is a falsity. What you are actually showing is stubbornness and a focus on ritual over intelligence.

Self-care takes all kinds of shapes and sizes, and there is no one-size-fits-all, but as a leader it is required of you to put an emphasis on it and demonstrate that it matters. Happy, cared for, well-adjusted people make better decisions, and better decisions lead to better companies and better products. And all that starts with your decisions and positioning of your vacation and leave policies.

## TIMING OF MESSAGING

This is by far the most egregious of all the endocrine-style signaling. If you have ever received a nine p.m. email from a boss, you know exactly where this is going.

When you send five a.m. or midnight emails to your team, whether you intend to or not, you are signaling your commitment to and expectations of the company or team. You are communicating an "always on" message that over time can and will infect your team.

I want to be very clear—there is nothing wrong with working on your own schedule. If you are a night owl and get some of your best thinking done at night, you should feel free to do so. But communicating to your team that that is your choice and not an expectation is critical. The signal that is sent when you send those messages at clearly non-working hours is a dangerous one, and one that can alienate your team from you, especially if you are a CEO or executive. Consider setting your emails to be sent in the a.m., just before the workday begins. This way, you can work when you are most productive and give your employees the benefit of having the time they are supposed to be off to be truly off.

Doing this also sets you up for another signal, one you want to be more paracrine like—when you DO send an email off-hours, it can create a sense of urgency when necessary, as opposed to being seen as "here we go again."

The other thing to consider with the timing of your messages is the time in which you actually reply to them in comparison to when they are sent. This is true for email and messaging alike.

As a leader, you owe it to yourself and to your team to take a breath before responding to every request or question. Your team (and potentially board or investors) relies on you to make the right decision, not the fast one. So, when you are faced with something that requires your attention, give yourself the right amount of time to answer. Over time, if your team sees that you respond to every request immediately, it signals to them not only that the expectation is immediacy but also that these decisions don't require airtime.

For a long time in my career I choose speed, believing that it made my teams feel heard when I responded to them instantly. And while they did feel like they had my attention at all times, what they didn't know is they didn't always have all of it. And I can tell you from experience they are better served with all your attention when you can give it than some of your attention immediately.

## BAGEL F**KING FRIDAYS

Unlike the other sections contained within "Endocrine Signals," I am going to be the opposite of objective on this topic.

Before I dive in, let me make perfectly clear that this is not specifically about bagel Fridays. I love bagels. And I love Fridays. And there is absolutely nothing wrong with having bagels on Fridays. What this is actually about is the laundry list of "work perks" that have been thrown into the mix when creating a company culture. Foosball tables, ping-pong tables, video game rooms, Kegerators, massage tables, cold brew stations, shoeshines, haircuts—and the list goes on and on and on.

Inherently there is absolutely nothing wrong with anything I listed. If you are in a position to afford those kinds of "perks" for your employees, you should feel free to. If you can buy lunch for your team weekly, do it. If you can shower your team with IPAs and cocktails on Fridays, have at it. But the messaging is everything. Absolutely everything.

I have had so many colleagues talk to me about compensation packages from incredible companies where the list of these "work perks" is seemingly to die for. Who wouldn't want three catered meals a day, on demand massages once a week minimum, nap pods in case you overeat during one of your catered meals, and then all the newest VR gear you can throw a stick at to play with at your leisure? Someone who eventually wants to go home at night, that's who.

I have worked for companies that had some, if not almost all, of these things, and they truly were job perks. What I mean by "truly" is that they were not leveraged as guilt. And in order to ensure that you don't do that with these perks, you need to set strict and detailed guidelines around the things you provide and their intention.

Food is the easiest example always—hence the bagel Friday reference. Every meal can have ulterior motives if you choose to allow it to. If you do order bagels for the office, order enough for everyone. Ordering close to enough or just shy of enough creates a sense of urgency to get the bagels, getting people into the office early to ensure they get that poppy seed bagel while there is one left.

Lunch can be similar. If the expectation is that when you order lunch in everyone goes back to their desk to eat, you've missed the point. Instead, encourage everyone to sit together and have a meal. That needs to be the intention of bringing lunch.

Dinner is the worst. I have almost never truly seen a company offer dinner to employees that wasn't at least somewhat of a ploy. It's either ordered late, which means people are likely at their desk working away until it shows up, or it's dropped off at your desk, all but guaranteeing you eat it there to avoid the guilt you would have in walking out of the office carrying it. Outside of taking people out to dinner where it is clearly not about getting you to work, or if you are throwing some kind of hack-a-thon or fun event where people are clearly aware that the intention is to have a working dinner, ordering dinner for your team will probably suck.

Just like the others, this is not a clear signal but one that over time, if not given the time and attention needed to clearly codify the message throughout the organization, can put you in a corner. There is absolutely nothing wrong with wanting the work environment to be fun. There is absolutely nothing wrong with wanting to provide extras for your team. But before you hit submit on any purchase, ask yourself the very real question of "Is this as close to a selfless act as there can be?" And if you have to take a real pause, maybe think it through a bit more.

## IN SUMMARY

Everything you do can and will have an impact on your culture and your product. As a leader, you need to be more aware than anyone else in your organization as to the kind of signals you are sending out on a regular basis. Your team are looking to you for guidance and approval at every turn, so being mindful of not only what you say but also what you do is beyond important.

You are going to make mistakes, and that's okay. It's actually wonderful. As we are about to discuss, being human is at the center of everything you do. As Alexander Pope said, "To err is human, to forgive is divine."

In order to stay aware of these signals, you need to have people around you who can be honest at all times. This is more about you as a leader and less about them as people. Identify individuals on your team who can sense when something might not have been perceived well and encourage them to come to you. When they do, never defend what you did. People's perception cannot be questioned. Just like in biology, the only way to dismiss a previous signal is with a new signal. So instead of reacting hastily and defensively, focus on the signal you want to send and make a point of doing so when you next have the opportunity.

Taking Action – With both paracrine- and endocrine-type signals, it is the consistency with which they are sent that increases the awareness of them. So, early on in the process of building your culture, write down the tenets you want to lead by and make note of them. If you can, create a Mantra for yourself that keeps you focused on your communication strategy as opposed to focusing on individual communication types. Keeping your focus on the big picture will allow you to stay present in the smaller moments (paracrine) and remain consistent with the larger courses you have likely already set (endocrine).

The single most important thing to never lose sight of when building a product or Product culture is that you are human, you will hire and work with humans, and what you are making will benefit humans.

# Be Human

## 14

T he single most important thing to never lose sight of when building a product or Product culture is that you are human, you will hire and work with humans, and what you are making will benefit humans.

This is harder than it sounds. It sounds pithy and like it might slowly be heading toward the "woo-woo" space. It might even sound like its heading into self-help land. For some people it might be both those things; for others who dabble in the "woo-woo" world, it likely won't. But this part of building Product and Product culture is the one thing in this book you cannot fake, and you cannot skip, or you will fail. Period.

Everything I have covered up to this point has been linked to relationships. It starts with your relationship to the product and how you will be able to best act as the captain of the ship. It then extends to the people you hire and work with who will be charged with helping to build the product itself. Then you need to consider the relationships with the people who you need to integrate with to launch your product. And finally, you get to the very people who are going to use your product. All the things we covered above, be it strategies or decisions or toolsets or messaging, are about successfully managing multiple relationships across all kinds of potential skill sets to ensure progress toward a common goal. But there is one relationship left, and it's the most important one: your product and your company's' relationship with the world.

Just like anyone else who is a "builder," you're going to introduce something either entirely new or different into the world. With that comes a very real responsibility. Unfortunately, specifically in the digital world, that responsibility was wildly ignored for a long time.

As a thought experiment, let's take a minute to think about bridges. As a product person, bridges are nothing short of absolute modern marvels to me, all the time. The Arkadiko, or Kazarma, Bridge is a Mycenaean bridge near the modern road from Tiryns to Epidauros on the Peloponnese, Greece. It is one of the oldest known arch bridges in the world, dating all the way back to the thirteenth century. When you look at it through today's eyes, it's nothing special. It's a bunch of rocks stacked on top of each other that allows for a crawl space below and passage on top. But when I look at it, all I can think about is how many times they likely attempted to build that bridge and failed. How many times did the rocks crumble when pressure was applied? How many formations did they attempt before they finally landed on one that was stable?

When looking at bridges today, they are astonishing. There are beam bridges, compression and tension bridges, suspension bridges—all different ways to complete a seemingly simple enough task. And the fact that in modern times these architects take the time to not only create them but build them to be stunning pieces of art is nothing short of miraculous.

However, let's not forget that there is a very real, tangible outcome to any kind of neglect when building a bridge. When architecting a bridge, "close enough" will not do. You need to be as near to perfection as possible every time or the consequences are dire. The weight of life literally rests in your hands.

That level of attention to detail and that gravity rarely exists in the digital realm. And if you look at the landscape of digital products, it shows. It's not that companies or individuals are careless, because in my experience that is not the case. But the idea that there is a safety net inherently changes the way you approach a problem. And so, the very knowledge that you can always roll code back can decrease the severity and pressure felt when putting something into the world. There is a fleeting nature to all things digitally built, almost like even while building it you know it's like vapor: visible for a moment and then gone.

And that's the trap. That innate sense of impermanence can fool you into compromising your morals, minimizing the impact of your decisions, and losing your center as a human. If you allow it to, it will be the death of your product and the death of your company.

The promise of digital to the world is access, connection, and parity. Those are the things that the digital space could allow us all to experience. We can make things safer, smarter, simpler, and more accessible. But the digital world is fast moving. We have innovated on the technology that builds technology so quickly that we cannot fully comprehend the true impact of that we build. It is, in some ways, too easy to build things.

For that reason, as the owner of a product, it is your responsibility as a human to zoom out regularly and look at the thing or things you are building from a broader worldview.

Prior to diving into this, I want to be clear that this does not mean you should not be competitive. It is very specifically your job to attempt to crush the competition in your space, and you should take that job very seriously. In doing so, it is still important to take stock of the actual "it" that you are building, and how your product fits in the larger world. So, you should make it a regular practice to ask yourself the following questions:

I.     Does what I'm making do anyone or anything harm?

It's important to note that this doesn't read "Does what I'm making do something good?" What you create doesn't have to be for the enrichment of the universe. It can be a mindless video game or a tactical API in service of a boring something or other, and that's totally fine. The question very specifically is does what you're making do something bad. This is a complicated matter to approach.

Basically, everything that exists in the digital world, much like the physical world, has both good and bad qualities. But the responsibility you should assume when creating a digital product is to weigh the good and the bad frequently and do your best to mitigate the bad.

Video gaming is a great example. Video games themselves have tons of scientifically proven advantages for children. They improve hand-eye coordination, improve visual and auditory memory, encourage focus and concentration, and even result in increased cognitive speed. The other side of that is that they can distract from genuine social interaction, can artificially inflate the need for competition, and can distract from other important growth activities. The Nintendo Wii had a brilliant, simple solution to this problem. During extended game play, the Wii would message users, "It's time to take a break," and tell them the game would pause for them. While a simple example, it's a strong use case of a product being aware of its true impact on the users and the world.

A less successful example would be the creation of "bots," or digital robots that can complete either a task or series of tasks. The idea of bots is a very attractive one—teach a computer program to perform menial tasks that are, quite literally, robotic, in order to free humans up to focus on tasks that genuinely require critical thinking. Unfortunately, bots are also a playground for doing extraordinarily shady and shitty things.

"Bot farms" spun up almost simultaneously with the larger acceptance of bots. These farms would tear through advertisements, surveys, or anything else that could be easily predicted. Millions, if not billions, of dollars were basically stolen from advertisers for "views" of advertisements that were, in fact, just bots scrolling through a page. And because of such nefarious activities, the world of bots has been slow to be adopted for the actual good they could do.

You cannot control the fact that there will always be bad actors. And unlike architecting and building a bridge, the barrier to entering the digital space is almost non-existent. So, if you are building digital products focused on bot technology, what do you do? It's not your fault that others choose to go rogue, right?

What you can do, and should do, is become part of the solution. In building your own technology, pay attention to where and how the software could be manipulated to perform ill-intentioned actions. Share your findings with the world, and loudly. In order to legitimize your product, you need to make your potential customers/users aware and protected against those who are using the technology for bad. It's not easy, and it won't always make you friends. It also will be a test of your and your team's resolve to be good humans yourselves, because I can tell you firsthand, if you work in the digital world long enough you are bound to come across something you could take advantage of.

That's why this question is so important. That's why you need to ask it of yourself and your team often. Getting yourself paid is a wonderful thing. Building a product that gets other people paid is an amazing feeling. Doing so at the cost of integrity and what's right is not, and in the long run it will do you no justice.

**II.** Is there a way to accomplish what my product sets out to do in a way that either more positively or less negatively impacts the ecosystem it exists in?

This question is a painful one, specifically if you don't ask yourself early in the process. The digital world is littered with discrete ecosystems. From social to gaming to finance to health, all these digital worlds operate with their own rules and regulations. Very often they will even all operate within similar technology stacks.

So, part of your responsibility is to take the ecosystem into account when you build your product. And while that sounds like a no-brainer, doing the right thing here is actually really hard.

Let's look at finance and health as examples. Due to the sensitive nature that both of those ecosystems deal with, they have been significantly slower to adopt new technologies. The risk of moving away from something that works (or is believed to work) is huge, so both these industries have rightfully played it safe.

Enter your new product. The easy thing to do, without question, would be to use whatever technology your potential ecosystem uses now, because otherwise you will be unable to break through and become a player in the space. Let's assume that there are significantly better technologies that do what your product is intending to do. Then what? The easy answer here is to conform and try to slowly change it from the inside. The fact is that has rarely worked. The true right thing to do is to do the right thing. That might mean you build your product or software exactly as you know it should be built, with the full understanding that you will need to build adaptors or supporting technology that can accommodate existing architecture.

What that means in real life is more time, more resources, more maintenance and support, and more capital. If you have ever raised money, built a digital product, or run a digital company, each of those words drove the dagger deeper into your heart. But if you are true to the mission of great product people and great product companies, you will do what is ultimately right, not what it easy. That's what bridge builders have to do. It's not a moral high ground when there is true risk involved, and more and more we have learned that protecting users' identities and data is a non-trivial pursuit.

So even though this question will more often lead to you banging your head against a desk than it will to popping champagne, to be a good digital citizen and to make the kind of impact on the world you should want to, you need to ask it.

**III.** Would I put my name on the door?

If this was the last thing you ever built, would you want it named after you? Do you have that kind of pride and belief in the thing you made?

I am a huge fan of stand-up comics. Stand-up comedians are the ultimate product people. Their entire purpose is to create something people enjoy and that enriches their lives while in real time interpreting feedback and adjusting the course as necessary to ensure they achieve their goal. They work tirelessly on the smallest things because they understand that every tiny detail builds into the larger premise and is necessary for a joke to really work. It takes years to hone the craft to the point that you are really incredible at stand-up, which is why there are an ungodly number of comedians and only a handful you can name.

You know what every comic has in common? Their name is on the special. Every. Single. Time. You can't escape attaching yourself to your comedy—you are a large part of the product. For that reason, comedians put in the work to ensure that when it moves out of tiny clubs and road tours and onto film, it is crisp, it is clean, and it is damn near perfect. Because if it's not, it's your name that will get dragged.

John Mulaney is one of the best stand-ups in the world right now. In 2015 he was given the opportunity to create a sitcom on Fox. He named it "Mulaney." It was critically dragged from the instant it aired. This man was recognized not just by popular opinion but by comics themselves to be one of the best working comics. His skits on Saturday Night Live are the stuff of legend. The two specials he put out prior to his show were hits even before the comedy boom. And yet his show failed, and it had his name on it. On Jerry Seinfeld's show, *Comedians in Cars Getting Coffee,* Mulaney talks about his mother having to read press that "Mulaney sucks."

*Mulaney* is the perfect example of true ownership and is the kind of thought process I am alluding to with this question. If that was the last thing John Mulaney ever did, there would be no denying it. He gave the show his actual name.

That's the kind of pride you want to build a product and product culture with. You want to create something that you not only are not afraid to put your name on, but that you would be proud to.

Sticking with the comedy world, there is no shortage of material about law firms that have fifteen names as the company moniker. When you become a partner at a law firm, it is rarely about pride. That kind of having your name on the door is almost always exclusively about ego. That's not what you should be looking at here.

When you ask yourself this question, it is not about making sure they spell your name right on the Pulitzer. It's not about being in Forbes 40 under 40. It's about the work and the work only. Did you not only create a product or a company that you are proud of and would want your name attached to, but did you do it the right way.

The "human" element in building successful products and companies is so often overlooked. The digital world has been built on insane work ethics and even more insane acquisition numbers. These "unicorn" success stories have become legends that, aside from at this point being so exaggerated that there is no doubt they are mostly full of shit, also set a very dangerous course for everyone who came after them.

Your product's place in the world will be a reflection of how it was built. Even if it is in the smallest ways, even if you build something consumed by very few, the mentality used to build something is visible in the end product practically every time.

The absence of a physical product does not mean the absence of impact on human beings. More and more digital products are playing roles in our lives that are crucial and critical. For that reason alone, it is increasingly important that you take the time to truly assess your product from a meaningful, human standpoint. If you don't, you can be sure others will, and in the digital age, your name will be attached to it . . .

If that was the last thing John Mulaney ever did, there would be no denying it. He gave the show his actual name. That's the kind of pride you want to build a product and product culture with.

Building digital companies
and products is a team sport.

It doesn't matter how good
you are.

It doesn't matter how many
skill sets you master.

To build something in the digital world that is designed
to serve many and scale, you
need other people's help.

# Essential Strategies: The Ultimate TL;DR Guide

**15**

I f you made it this far, what you have read is a collection of things that I have learned through years of observation, successes, and abject failures. I have tried to outline the considerations and steps you need to take to best set yourself up for success. I have also tried to do so in far less words than you are supposed to use in a book, because writing a book about creating meaningful products intelligently and then drawing that out felt like it flew directly in the face of the premise.

Over time I have personally come to appreciate things that I can use as "north stars." As you have surely observed by this point, I like catchy one-liners and quick stories to prove points. Having an appreciation for the past has always been important to me. But having read Desk Reference Guides and all other sorts of business-style literature, I also know that the speed with which the digital world moves simply will not allow for you to reread all the brilliant things that have been written to keep yourself oriented.

For that reason, I have tried to consolidate a lot of the messages written in this book into a list of <u>twelve</u> quick-hitter items that you can easily reference when you feel like you're in a jam, need to reorient, or even just want to remind yourself that you're not alone when you get in the weeds.

This is not a cheat sheet. If you have learned one thing throughout reading this book, I hope it is that there is no cheating when building a great product or company—it takes time and thoughtfulness and energy and focus. But in the world of "too long didn't read" and having been in a position where I have had no choice but to skim things, this felt like the right thing to do. So away we go . . .

## BUILDING DIGITAL COMPANIES AND PRODUCTS IS A TEAM SPORT

It doesn't matter how good you are. It doesn't matter how many skill sets you master. To build something in the digital world that is designed to serve many and scale, you need other people's help. Hard stop. There will be minutes, days, potentially even weeks where you will think to yourself, "I would be better off just doing all of this myself." But I am here to tell you definitively that that is not the case. Physical products that seem entirely singular are, in fact, not. Before you can make a bracelet or a ring, someone needs to source the metal, cut the metal, source the stones, create the tools you use to create the shape, etc. The "invisible line" of things that got done prior to your being able to make something in the physical world exists in the digital world too.

Also, even if you did amass design, product, development, and quality assurance skills, it's likely you're not the best at all four of them. Having more eyes on a product is never a bad thing, and collaboration, in my experience, is what always results in the best output. So, build a team you can trust, and then trust them.

## FALL IN LOVE WITH "I DON'T KNOW BUT I'LL FIND OUT"

As we just discussed, it is unlikely you are a four-tool player in digital products. What's important is that you are aware of that fact, own it, and are comfortable with it. "I don't know but I'll find out" might very well be the most important phrase you can use when building a company or a product.

This is true for two main reasons:

I.     You don't know everything, and that is okay.

Seriously. It's fine. If you did know everything you would be insufferable anyway. Get and stay very comfortable with the aspects of your product you don't know the nitty-gritty of. There is a reason you have a team, and there is a reason you built a company. Be willing to let their light shine where you are dark.

II.    Make sure people know that you know you don't know everything.

Leading a digital company or product team doesn't mean you have all the answers. It means you know how to make sense of the questions being asked and that you can get the answers to those questions. The idea that you show weakness when you have to admit you don't know something in front of your team, clients, partners, or users is an ego problem. There is weakness in suggesting you know something when you know deep down you don't. There is weakness in not trusting your team to be able to deliver an answer on your behalf. There is absolutely no weakness in not knowing.

## NO MEANS KNOW

When asked a yes or no question, you now understand that you actually have three possible answers. You can say "yes", you can say "I don't know but I'll find out", or you can say "no".

As a leader, "no" is something you need to get super familiar with. Inherently it's not a great-feeling word. It carries with it a negative connotation, and in your role as a leader can easily be viewed as a power move. You cannot allow any of that to waver your use of the word.

When you say no, what you really mean is "I know why that won't work." The reason could be time based, it could be resource based, it could be personality based—it honestly doesn't matter. What matters is that when you straight up say "No" to someone it needs to be clear to them, and to you, that you mean it and have a genuinely good reason for saying it.

No is not a bad word when it comes from someone you trust. It can come to mean "not yet" or "not without more discussion," both of which are super healthy. And if you can add those addendums to a no, genuinely you should feel free to do so. But if, and only if, you mean it. They cannot be used as a crutch, and they are not a replacement for the hard no. Being frank and firm is your job as a leader. Don't make someone else be the "No-person."

Own the role, stand behind it, and always be willing to listen to the argument against it.

## PROCESS FIRST

Before you can build anything, you need to know how you are going to build it. And not just a rough idea. This deserves the airtime to be truly thought through.

You're excited to get to work. This idea is an awesome one and you simply cannot wait to see it come to life. I know. But first, process. The amount of time it takes you to think through these beforehand pales in comparison to the amount of time you will spend fixing both the lack of process and the product itself if you do not.

If you are unsure about how to set the processes up, ask for help. Look to advisors, look to friends or colleagues, reach out to people who have successfully done this before. The absence of reasonable and thoughtful process has been, and will continue to be, the downfall of so many companies and products. Take the time to do it right; trust me.

## PATIENCE IS A VIRTUE, AND SPEED IS AN ELEMENT

You can't measure patience. It will be a constant pain point for you as you build your company and your product. How long is too long? Is this patience or is this lackadaisical?

Waiting is hard. Ask any three-year-old who has been in the car for more than fourteen consecutive minutes. But it is your job to not only have patience but encourage it throughout the entirety of your team and your company. You built this team, you built this process—you have to trust it. So, if things are taking longer than you had planned, remain patient but persistent.

Creating a culture that is not patient will inevitably turn into a culture that rewards speed over accuracy and precision. With client-driven products, this is sometimes a trade that might need to be made. However, setting this precedent is dangerous, because in a world where people have less and less tolerance for non-working products, the number of times you can ship something that "kinda" works is limited. Be mindful of that and make it your mission to make everyone around you mindful of that as well. Long-term, you are talking about a prodigious payout.

## HARDER DOES NOT MEAN CORRECT

The digital world is in a constant state of evolution. It is forever expanding and contracting. For that reason, specifically when it comes to development, you will constantly be in a position of making decisions around how you do certain things.

For some reason, in my experience, often the thing that is more challenging to do is presumed to be the right thing. Sometimes it very well might be, but being hard does not make it correct. It might just be the first way the team agreed would work. It might be that even though it is more work, it is work that is done within a framework or codebase that is more familiar to the team. But in neither of those situations is it actually the right answer.

Engineers' brains are amazing machines. Their capacity for problem-solving is nothing short of astounding, and it will be the thing that makes you succeed. But without guidance and reasoning it can also overcomplicate solutions. Even when you feel out of your depth, make sure you are getting full explanations as to why decisions are being made. Never be afraid to ask the "stupid" question. Not being able to develop something yourself does not make you unable to solution with the team. Engineering is logic based, and as it is your job to never lose site of the product's north star, you are in a prime position to steer your team toward that destination. Do so without fear.

## ZOOM OUT

Cherish this saying. Seriously. You will need it all the time. It is easily one of the most commonly spoken collections of words that comes out of my mouth.

As the leader of your company or product, you are squarely in charge of keeping track of what the larger goal and purpose is. Even the best intentions and most talented teams are likely to get blinders on at some point in order to get a particular task done. If you are not present and loud in reminding the team to "zoom out" and keep focus on the larger picture, you have failed.

Zooming out is also a phenomenal way to ensure you remain user-centric at the very core of your company or product. If you always zoom out to look at the problem, you are addressing things from the user's view, and will be able to quickly determine the amount of brain capacity and energy that the conversation deserves. To no fault of any engineer or designer, I have very often been able to get to a moment of "this is not worth this amount of time" by simply employing the zoom out method. It is a great reminder to the team and to yourself why you are all actually here.

## DON'T BUILD CEMETERIES

I have always hated the idea of cemeteries. They are the ultimate egoist move. Even when you have given all your life to the world, you require a monument in your honor to remind everyone that you existed.

Regardless of whether you agree or not, I cannot stress how much you should not build cemeteries within your organization. I have seen many companies and teams that have references and reminders of products long defunct, phased out, trashed, or retired under the guise of "learn from where we have been." Your team does not to be reminded. Building monuments to things past will only shine a light on how good things were or create animosity for the work that needed to be done to get away.

Remembering the past is important, but celebrating it or throwing up your middle finger toward it is a fool's errand. It is your job to be present in the here and now with an eye to the future. Historical context is always meaningful, but that story is already written. Write the pages of the story you are in now and write them in such a way that you are heading toward how you want the story to end. Every time you take a break to admire or admonish the past, all you are doing is hitting pause on the present.

## REALISTIC ROADMAPS FOR THE WIN

There is no magic period of time that you should be able to report on at any given moment as to exactly what and exactly how you will be building a thing. That idea comes from a world and a time that did not move at the pace of the world you live in.

I encourage you to have an aspirational roadmap. Talking about big goals and where you want to go is hugely important for you as the leader, and for your team. Building blindly deliverable to deliverable is zero fun. You need to have a direction and some kind of endgame.

You also need to be realistic about how far into your future is reasonable to plan for and at what level of depth. Different industries within digital allow for different timetables, so be mindful of your particular world. But also, do not be afraid to keep things high-level at a certain point. If you get pushback, stand your ground and ask the aggressor what they are having for dinner three weeks from the following Tuesday. They know they are going to eat. They likely know where in the world they will be. That level of specificity is appropriate for that time frame. Knowing more than that would not only be a strange thing to be aware of, but also highly subject to change. And that's exactly why you should feel confident in planning only as far out and as deeply as makes sense for your business, and no more.

## ASK WHY MORE

"Why" is a powerful tool. In your role as a leader, "why" can quite literally save your company or your product. And unlike with "no," you should use it with absolutely reckless abandon.

No matter what kind of skill set you have or who you're talking to, you should never feel like asking why is not appropriate. Understanding the thought process and logic behind the decisions made for your product will become your superpower. When you continuously ask why, you relieve the need to be in the depths of every minute decision. Instead, by confirming that the reason behind the decision is in line with the larger picture and organizational mindset, you can allow your teams the freedom to operate without you meddling.

## what

Every organization on the planet knows WHAT they do. These are products they sell or the services

## how

Some organizations know HOW they do it. These are the things that make them special or set them apart from their competition

## why

Very few organizations know WHY they do what they do, WHY is not about making money. That's a result. WHY is a purpose, cause or belief. It's the very reason your organization exists

The Golden Circle

what

how

why

It is the ultimate product tool. Simon Sinek's famous TED Talk explains his "Golden Circle." At the very center of the circle is "Why." Mr. Sinek defines "Why" as the purpose, cause of belief. If you can orient your organization to think about "Why" in that context and answer the question when you ask it with that definition in mind, you have successfully created a product—and likely user—minded company. Congrats.

## STRUGGLE PORN IS REAL

Nat Eliason wrote a brilliant piece on Medium in October of 2018 titled "No More Struggle Porn." Nat brilliantly outlines that while entrepreneurship and business is hard, struggling is not. He goes on to define "struggle porn" as "a masochistic obsession with pushing yourself harder, listening to people tell you to work harder, and broadcasting how hard you're working."

The digital world has been a continual battleground of "struggle porn wars," in my opinion. People making it widely known the endless hours and exorbitant resources they have dedicated to their product. Missing from many of those claims, however, is success.

Think about NBA players. If you are 5'9", put in endless hours at the gym, work on your game nonstop, and are in peak physical condition, the likelihood you will ever play for an NBA team is slim to none. Out of 3,071 players, only 25 of them have been 5'9 or under; that's .008 percent.

The point here is that just working hard is not enough. The product itself has to actually fix a problem or solve an unmet need, and you need to be working on it the right way. If you find yourself working endless hours, driving your team into the ground, and are getting nowhere, you need to not buy into "struggle porn" science. If you are in that situation, you either have a product problem, a process problem, or both. At that point, you owe it to yourself and your team to listen and prescribe to another product gospel tenant, zoom out.

As Albert Einstein famously did not say (it was actually author Rita Mae Brown who penned the quote), "Insanity is doing the same thing over and over and expecting different results." That's where you end up with "struggle porn." If your organization and product are on the struggle bus, don't chalk it up to "them's the ropes." Figure it out and fix it or face a hard truth.

## REAL ARTISTS SHIP

Steve Jobs is one of the more polarizing individuals in the digital world. He was a literal visionary, able to see things that simply didn't exist and bring them into the world. He was also, by many accounts, a dick. And while I personally could take or leave a lot of the Apple lore, he did say one thing that has been on my desk in some capacity for years now: "Real artists ship." This is an idea that I hold very true, and one that I believe is paramount for any aspiring Entrepreneur or Product Leader.

There are lots of theories about what Jobs meant when he said this. For me, the message has always been clear. Ideas are the easy part. Coming up with something that excites you, that would make your life easier or better, is not overly difficult. Having the wherewithal to think it all the way through, understand it from every angle, create the company and the processes to be able to execute on it, and eventually execute on it is an entirely different story.

That part takes dedication. That part takes sacrifice. Getting to that part is what makes you an artist. Building great digital companies and products is no different than anything else. If it was easy, everyone would do it. And when you think about the accessibility we have in the digital world, it's amazing there are not more great digital products. The reason there aren't? It's hard work. And it takes groups of people working together to make truly great digital products. So, when you fall in love with a new idea, or a new feature, or a new product line, always keep in mind that ideas are easy, and execution is hard. Real artists ship products.

Live and Die by "The Shopping Cart" Theory

At the end of the day, building a company and a product all comes down to people. The kind of leader you choose to be, the kind people you hire, the kind of people you don't hire, and the kind of people whose world you are trying to improve with your product.

As a quick and easy tool, always remember the shopping cart theory. The theory is a rather simple one. It states that a shopping cart is the ultimate litmus test for whether a person is a positive or negative influence on their surroundings. When you bring a shopping cart out to your car in the parking lot, to return that shopping cart is objectively right. Outside of either physical inability or very unusual extenuating circumstances, there is no reason not to bring the shopping cart back to the shopping cart return. There is no punishment for not bringing the shopping cart back. No laws are broken, no fines will be handed out. The worst thing you might get is a passing glare or in rare instances a mumbled "really dude?" under an onlooker's breath. But the only reason you bring the shopping cart back to the shopping cart return is because you know it's the right thing to do.

And that minorly inconveniencing yourself saves someone else the trouble of having to. Because regardless of whether you bring it back or not, it will be brought back. This is the shopping cart theory.

When building your team and your culture, the single best thing you can do is hire people who would return the shopping cart every time. That sense of morality and of doing what's right even when no one is watching is what building great products is all about: helping.

**Real artists ship.
Ideas are the easy part.**

Coming up with something that excites you, that would make your life easier or better, is not overly difficult. Having the wherewithal to think it all the way through, understand it from every angle, create the company and the processes to be able to execute on it, and eventually execute on it is an entirely different story.

# Of all the things discussed in this book, one theme runs true through every single page— be good and do good.

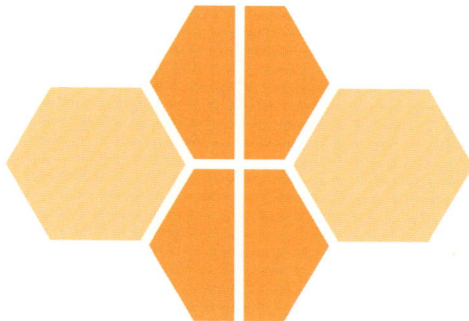

# Parting Thoughts 16

There is so much potential beauty in the things that we can create in the digital world. We are still in the infancy of understanding how all this incredible technology is shaping our now, let alone our future. What I hope this book has done is provided you with a map and a compass. The map is expansive, and there is a ton of uncharted territory I can't fill in for you. The compass is a tool that will always orient you, but it is up to you the paths you choose.

I have been so incredibly lucky to work with people who helped define my map and orient my compass. It is because of these people that I have the opinions I expressed in this book. It is because of their willingness to fail, willingness to share in success, willingness to be patient, and most of all, willingness to trust that I have been able to hone my compass to the place that it is now.

Of all the things discussed in this book, one theme runs true through every single page—be good and do good. All of the recommendations in this book are centered around the philosophy that making things easier for the people around you will positively impact them, and therefore positively impact the process and the product or company you build. If you take nothing else from this, please walk away with the knowledge that your willingness and capacity to do right by other people will be the thing that is remembered far after your product vanishes from the digital realm.

Put your shopping cart back.

# Acknowledgements

I first started the process of writing this book at the end of 2019. I had no idea what the next year would bring, and had no idea what I was doing. Luckily there was a small army of people who came to my aid, kept me moving forward, whom without none of this would have ever come to fruition.

**Tom Goodwin** was someone I looked up to long before I got to call him a friend. He was the very first person who read the outline of this book, and he said a line that was simultaneously one of the nicest things anyone ever said to me and abjectly terrifying - "I have bad news for you, you might be an author". Without your friendship, guidance and belief, this book is not real.

**Danny Nathan** kept this alive when it was close to dead. Believed in me, what I was writing and helped me figure out how to make it so. For that I am forever indebted.

**Maureen Garvey**, my first (and favorite) editor. If Deb could see your name in my book, she'd laugh if nothing else. Love you Mo.

**Jason Osburn** pushed me to make it personal, to curate the experience in a way I didn't see at first. Thank you for pushing me.

**Ryan Bricklemeyer**, who told me he wanted other people to read my book, which is the nicest thing anyone can say about your book.

**Jeffery Arnowitz**, who might have been the first person to read the whole thing. He then gave notes on the whole thing - notes that made me recognize what I actually wanted to do here.

**Jeremy Toeman** let me do this while we started a company. He let me build it, the community around it, and he reminded me daily I was good at this product thing.

**Robert Gwyn Palmer**, who was so much more than just an agent. Through rewrites, edits, a pandemic, a title change, he was steadfast not only in his being but in his belief, without which this book surely never gets published.

**Ingrid "Iggy" Husby** made this book FEEL like I wanted it to. No... like I needed it to. To be able to have this much fun while creating is all I ever want for people. Thank you for making it fun and beautiful all at the same time.

**Mom and Dad**, Vince and Nance, Tutu and Yoda. You go by many names, everyone one of which has led to this life I live being possible. Thank you for continued, unwavering and relentless support.

**Kayla**, since the day I met you everything I made is because of you in some way. You inspire me to be a version of myself I never saw (and still sometimes struggle to). Your willingness to take this ride is something I don't think I will ever be able to truly thank you for, so this will have to do. Thank you LB.

**Lennon and Charlie**, you are now and will forever be, without question, the best things I will ever have anything to do with. I hope for both of you that you find a passion that encourages you to explore it the way I had to explore mine in the pages in this book. I hope that you grow up in a space that allows you to believe you can build the kind of life you want, with the kind of people you want. I hope you hear me in these pages and smile. I love you Jellybean. I love you Bear.